The Other Genders

Androgyne Genderqueer Non-Binary Gender Variant

Intergender, Mixed Gender, Ambigender, Agender, Neutrois, Nullgender, Bigender, Multigender, Plural Gender, Fluid Gender, Third Gender, Gender Outlaw, Pangender, Polygender, Omnigender, Pregender, Postgender, Self-Defined Gender, Unlabeled Gender, Outside the "Box" Gender, Gender Blended, and other

Infinitely Defined Genders

By Ken Wickham (aka Kendall, Kendra, KK)

Contents

2

Acknowledgments

I acknowledge that this book is for all the Androgynes/Genderqueers/Non-Binary Gender Variants "the others" that want a voice, want issues recognized, and want a presence in culture. I hope it will bring some understanding, further questioning, greater research, more respect, equal treatment from others, and greater awareness of the our existence.

Rebis, Stephe Feldman, MiaAndMarq (M&M), Pica Pica (Youtube video master), Zythyra (y2gender, Z),Laurry, ChildOfTheLight, Sparkles, Elwood, Cobalt (Alison), JC, Thoenix (Tay) Jaimey, Casey, Seshatneferw, Nicole (Nicksister), Andra, Doc, nyeti nyeti (jan c), PoeticVengeance (Sophia), Kaimialana (Kai, Kaimi, Alana), static_nonsense (error, kay, zero), Kai'enne, Simon, Alexthesane, Kinkly, Silverblue, Emerald, Catechin, Wesley_Lexi , Gwydion, Jamie, Sky, Louise, Attis, no_id, Veetje

Steph, Cindi Jones, Tink, Alice, Chaunte, Jillieann
And last but not least Nero (our adopted FtM).

"Other" Gender

"Other" gender. This is how many people that don't fit into traditional binary gender categories and labels are referred to in many current writings. Whether its polls, surveys, studies, or applications filled out for whatever reason, the "other" is constantly present.

Within this "other" is a wealth of diversity, many times unnamed, sometimes named by others, a few times with similar community type labels, sometimes even rejecting labels all together choosing to stay out of the "boxes".

How does one know one is an other gendered person?

Normally it all begins, many times at a very young age, when one feels different then all the others surrounding them. Sie may feel not fitting in with the others. Not just on a getting-along basis. Rather than on a deep level that deals with one's identity. Sie may feel that hir actual identity of hir gender is supposed to be both/neither male or female, outside of gender, third gender, beyond gender, absence of gender, mixed gender, changing gender, or all genders.

These other gender feelings may continue on throughout adolescence onto adulthood. Along the way to adulthood obstacles may arise. Very common among other gendered persons is deciding at these young ages to suppress one's natural person. Instead of allowing one to feel like another gendered person, one tries to fit in with all the other girls or guys. One tries to earnestly to hide, forget, change, or replace those natural feelings.

Feeling not belonging in one's assigned gender, nor in the opposite gender is another common experience shared by many. One may even seriously consider or even transition to the other sexual biology, though eventually one still feels that they don't belong in just one or the other. One poll of those identified as other gender resulted in half of those other genders (15 out of 40) as having extreme discomfort with one's birth gender and considered SRS or HRTi.

Feeling lost for a period of time, or even reoccurring later is a common feeling, Other genders are by far rare and uncommon. Sie cannot talk to just anyone about these feelings. And the chances of meeting another other gender at a young or even any age is extremely slim, especially prior to community groups specifically for other genders. And having no common path to travel, or having no path at all, increases such feeling of being lost.

One may experience troubles socially. Since one is trying to fake fitting in, one's natural abilities, reactions, and behavior doesn't quite come fluidly. This can lead to awkwardness and noticeable inhibitions or overacting. Social experiences can mirror such inabilities.

Many develop a habit of changing subjects and topics[ii] which can explain why many like to go on tangents often in conversations and writing, sometimes jumping topics. It is unknown why so many seem so unorganized and illogical[iii]. It may come from the constant dodging of gendered behavior, conversations, and activities of the earlier years. Always trying to get away from or hide one's true self.

One may learn to be silent. Saying nothing at all seems better than going against what seems to be an entire world. The risk of socially being placed as an outcast far seemly outweighs the benefits of speaking one's true feelings, yet being oneself.

With all the hiding, suppressing, silence, social awkwardness, changing subjects, feelings of being lost and not belonging, can lead to an up and down sense of esteem[iv] for one's true self, or a high fake sense of esteem but for a fake self. Its hard to feel good about oneself, or sense of self worth, when one is denying its very existence.

Pronouns fail. Hearing "mam","sir", "he", "she", and especially "it", may make them cringe. When one uses these two gendered, or similar pronouns, one is also labeling the person referred to, with a specific gender. Many people don't realize how powerful and debilitating the pronouns can be to other gendered persons. Nor the liberation of going beyond such gendered labels by not using them, or using alternatives.

One may feel the presence of two or more different gender persons within themselves. These individuals may have their own personalities, style of speaking, likes and dislikes, dialog, and own unique selves. They may have their own names.

And once one enters the path to trying to understand oneself, that path may be hard to find. Glimpses and partial similarities may be experienced from time to time, as if someone else has found the answer to your own journey. While others find out that paths followed were not meant for them,

One may adopt one label, to find out later that no longer applies, or something better matching has come along.

In order to exist with the other world, such as workplace, churches, communities, and school, one binary gender identity might have to be used with pronouns, despite one's natural resistance to a binary.

In all of this, one feels natural ungendered or nullgendered, pregendered, both or mixed gendered, outside gendered, postgendered, omnigendered. The rules don't seem to fit you.

Concerning Gender, everything you have learned your whole life from others, about you and the world, seems wrong.

This book focuses exclusively on non-binary gender identities.

How and why this book was made

The reason for this book comes basically from a comment, challenge, and goal set to me and others in a non-binary gender forum to bring, as "Rebis" asked twice in two different forums that I know of. This and a few other feelings I will share a bit later.

In a post a Susans.org. "We need to market ourselves ," by Rebis on November 05, 2007.

> Hi,
> The subject says it all. We need to market ourselves. To make ourselves better known to the world at large.
>
> Any ideas? I expect results.
>
> Rebis

Which a follow up post mentioned me though at the time I did not have plans beyond my Susans Androgyne FAQ. I am the KK, for Ken/Kendra which I was called for a nickname back then.

> ...I'm sure that **KK** and no_id and would be good contributors. They have orderly and functioning minds (by which I don't mean to imply that the rest of us are dolts).

I must say, at that time I had no ambition to make a book. I was very busy at the time with real life work.

The other post was at Whatisgender.net. "Gender Variant people need some serious PR/marketing," by Rebis on Mon Nov 19, 2007.

> My thinking is that as a group, androgynes/gender variants/genderqueers are relatively unknown. There are also people who do know of us, but refuse to recognize our issues. I believe that we need a presence in the overall culture and not just within the LBGT subculture where we seem to barely reside.
>
> Some of us have been working on youtube videos and I think that is a good idea. Other ideas I have is to design logos and such in order to get non-variants to ask about us.
>
> It would be really cool if somebody could get some articles written and published.

Anyway, what are your thoughts? What are your ideas?

Rebis

When I was doing some research for a major revision of my Androgyne FAQ in July (one day before my birthday), adding new sources, I came across some transgender material for a college transgender course. I read it, and was deeply dissatisfied. ᵥ Dissatisfied with the lack of Androgyne, Genderqueer, Non-Binary Gender information. The more I researched transgender material, the more I felt pushed aside, left as side notes, or quickly summarized with words such as "others", with some brief generalized statement.

This dissatisfaction lead me to buy $150 from the great god of the internet, Amazon.com, of the most non-binary gender books that I could find.ᵥᵢ With only a few exceptions, this in turn lead to a greater dissatisfaction.

So deciding to take up Rebis's call for help at helping get us known more, angered by what was available and having a FAQ with tons of useful information, I decided to go for it, and try my hand at something.

Conceptual Framework: Structure, Motivation, Claims, Questioning, Method, Reasoning, Obstacles

Question
What is non-binary gender and what are their issues?

Motivation: Comment, Challenge, Goal

"We need to market ourselves make ourselves known to the world non-binary gender persons do exist, and many wish to be heard and known in the world and communities.
- •Unknown
- •Seldom talked about in society... Use as a starting point to talk about non-binary.
- •Known, but don't recognize our issues
- •Writing & Published

Non-binary genders feel left out, avoided, and invisible. For the most part this is true.

Why does society know very little about non-binary genders? And can they know more about non-binary genders? Can one present evidence supporting claims concerning non-binary genders, despite the variety of identities and individualistic nature?

Find available information---> use as a starting point to start "talking" about non-binary genders.

So that others can know more about the other's genders or relate to their own gender identity, and learn more about both.

Major Sources whatisgender.net, susans.org, yahoo androgyne group lauras-playground.com [list in order of quality, significance, and importance]

Claim: Non-binary genders are worth talking, learning, and conversing about, and one can make sense, claims, and general statements concerning data. Non-binary genders are understandable, measurable, and have many shared characteristics, issues that many share, even despite in this diverse, individual, multiple, unique group of people and cultures, available from current data, which can lead to further investigation, research, conversations, and analysis.

<u>Primary method:</u> The primary method that I will use is combing for surveys, polls, and additional comments to those data sources. These sources are recorded in their natural state, in that I am not sending out requests to take surveys, nor organizing polls specifically for this writing. They are responding to polls on their own, many times anonymously. Despite this, there is room for error and misrepresentation. I do not assume this method to be perfect, though I do consider it reliable, consistent, and accurate, especially if I do so by taping multiple sources that produce similar results and information, or complementary results. Such multiple source comparison will be used when possible and available

<u>Problems and obstacles.</u> When you look for non-binary information, most of the time what you get is unreliable, biased, opinionated, unsupported information. This includes lists of non standard definitions and terminology (sometimes changing, multiple words for one concept, or similar concepts), filled with someone's personal opinion (sometimes critical, other times irrational), many times unsupported by facts, data, or reasoning. Many times transgender surveys and polls leave out options for additional genders.

Many times non-binary genders are pushed aside with general marginalizing,"and then there are those that feel like "other" genders statements, without further details. And then they talk about and focus on specific transsexual or crossdresser issues and characteristics, sometimes using the banner of transgender.

<u>Dual nature goals</u> is an attempt to find some of that information, or read into the information as much as possible. To lift that problematic barrier, if not answer a list of questions, at least lead one in a direction that one can go to pursue such answers. To answer or help lead one in direction of the answer.

<u>Current data and analysis</u>
What is the current known characteristics of non-binary?
    Birth Sex
    Body
    Presentation, Roles, Expression
    Orientations
    Coming Out

What is the current population of non-binary?
How accurate could the data be (sample size), based off of a logical derived population amount?

What types of non-binary are there? What are the individual nature and
characteristics of such types?
What are the aspects of one's life possibly affected by non-binary gender?
What obstacles do non-binary gender persons face?
What are the fears of non-binary?
How are non-binary gender persons treated unequally?
What are anti-non-binary stances and viewpoints?
What do non-binary gender persons call themselves? Why are names
important?
What is the modern history of non-binary genders?

Part 1 Introduction to Other Genders

Chapters 1 through 5

The back of the book has a topical index to supplement these chapters

How did you first encounter the word genderqueer

- Online Communities: 35%
- Online Research: 17%
- Friends/Support Groups: 14.6%
- Education/School: 13.6%
- Books: 3.9%
- Pop Culture: 3.9%
- Other: 11.7%

Poll retrieved May 14, 2011 from http://genderqueerid.com/

Chapter 1 An Introduction to Non-Binary (*Other*) Genders

As the preface mentions, knowledge of an other gendered persons, either of
*self or another person, is normally the first step in understanding, discussing,
researching, arguing for or against issues, or relating one's self to other
gender. Chapter one is an overall introduction and explores the extent.of other
genders.*

*Current data and information then can present a body of modern issues.
Chapter two begins to analyze such lists of information. Much of the data has
good correlation, is measurable, and is understandable despite gender's variety*

1.1 Are the "other"genders worth knowing about?

The "*other*" genders are worth knowing about. They most definitely bring
interesting new terms, dwell in realms of unconventional concepts, face
challenging real issues, possess diverse interests, and forces one to face day-
to-day identity and social definitions.

1.1.1 "Other" genders = non-binary genders

In this book "other" genders = non-binary genders, as well as a vast array of
words that fill this great expanse of cultures and identities.

1.1.2 What are some benefits of non-binary gender to society?

Their benefit to society can be positive. Their contribution to society need
not be scary, confusing, nor misunderstood. They can help others to feel
better about about oneself for being not just ultra masculine nor ultra
feminine. Rather to accept humans as being mixed in gender aspects, despite
one's biology. Even those that are not non-binary can appreciate the benefits
of living in a more non-binary world.

1.1.3 What can binary gender persons learn from non-binary genders?

So maybe by looking at those that identify as non-binary gender people, one
can learn to appreciate one's own gender identity and gender aspects. And
also one can look at others with a new perspective.

1.2 What is gender?

Gender is a category. Sometimes it is referred to as being a box. In
linguistics, it refers to a category words related to the gender of the speaker.
In fashion, it refers to a category of colors, material, shapes, styles, patterns,
and items used by that specific gendered person. In psychology and
sociology it refers to one's identity of the self, and one of the most basic
cultural groups one belongs to. Not only can one identify as a gender, society
can also place meaning and parameters upon that gender. A vast array of
expectations, rules, and limits are place on this basic cultural social group
and personal identity.

1.2.1 What is binary gender?

A *binary gender* refers to meaning there is masculine and feminine. These two categories come with some basic rules and assumptions. One is exclusively one or the other. One cannot be both. Many believe that it is based off of one's birth sex. Others believe that despite birth sex, one must be only one or the other. Some believe that one can change one's sex, to the opposite sex, though gender remains only binary. Binary gender doesn't see different degrees or mixtures of gender identity within people. There is no masculine women, nor feminine men. Binary gender does not believe in androgynous gender identities. Nor neutrality. Nor multiple gender identities within the same person.

1.2.2 Binary gender leads to what kind of expectations?

Binary gender expectations are a product of binary gender. These are sometimes called *gender norms*. These are the ideals that fit within the specific gender, created by societies and cultures, groups of people, for whatever reason.

A girl is....

A boy is....

A girl can do this....

A boy can do this....

A girl is supposed to be like this....

A boy is supposed to be like this....

Girls like....

Boys like....

Does this sound familiar?

1.2.3 What is non-binary gender?

Having said what binary gender means and what it's focus and limits are, what then is non-binary gender.

In it's most basic form, *non-binary gender* is not only being just one of these two genders. Which is to say, that being non-binary gender is not a binary gender only.

Some go on to specify subcategories that it could mean being both, neither, mixed, changing, multiple, self defined, beyond, unknown, infinite, or a third gender. Also, birth sex has a more minimal influence on one's non-binary gender, though some influence remains. One's non-binary gender may or may not influence some important aspects of gender such as one's behavior, gender roles, thinking, social identity, presentation (gender expression), and sex (birth or modified/changed). Fears, challenges, and obstacles socially and psychologically may be influenced by one's non-binary gender.

1.2.4 Are there limits and expectations to a non-binary gender person?

A non-binary person can have less limits and norms. They can choose for themselves what their own how their own limits are determined. The choices are endless.

A non-binary gender person is whatever they want, whatever feels right, and whatever is true. Their existence is defined by their own self.

1.3 What is the self?
At the center of everyone's existence, whether selfish or unselfish, is the *self*. I don't mean that everyone's most important thing is life is one's self. Rather that all first hand observations of reality taking place in real time, is perceived by individual's thoughts, awareness, focus, emotions, desires, needs, and active sensual reception, which we name this individual viewer the self.

Psychology has named the collection of the aspects of the self-identity the *self-schema* or *self-concept*. What this means is that there are many aspects, assessments, attributes, and response to stimulus that makes up who one is. Gender and gender identity are part of this self-concept. Though discrepancies can create problems in one's life, especially during child development.

1.3.1 Non-binary gender child development
As a child develops the child experiences moments of joy, pleasure, peace, and sense of freedom. These experiences happen at times when one is open to all gender behavior, sense of self, and with little inhibitions. Often one hears of experiences of one exploring or finding out something about themselves concerning gender or gender identity. Such experiences however is normally followed by some sort of inhibition.

1.3.2 Repression, suppression, and oppression
Unfortunately most societies and cultures have a way of looking down upon such open exploration or realizations. In addition, *social agents* such as parents, teachers, religious figures, relatives, neighbors, and peers have a way of enforcing gender behavior to let one know how they ought to or should be. After those moments of joyful natural personal experience more often than not, one experiences something or some social agent that forces one to inhibit such experience, a source of oppression. These may be direct or indirect forces. Realizing that one must hide, inhibit, "change", or suppress and repress those natural experiences leads one to temporary "fixes". One tries to avoid such feelings , emotions, and behavior in exchange for pretending to be something else, though with social rewards such as praise, recognition, and social status, and avoid social punishments of ridicule, violence, feelings of being low status, picked on, or feeling of being wrong.

1.3.3 Self-Discrepancies

Self-discrepancies can and do occur within non-binary gender people, as well as other transgender persons and people in general. Psychology has broken the self into current, ideal, and ought selves. When currently a person is one way, and then in their mind they have an ideal self image, one can experience great sadness, depression, dissatisfaction, and disappointment. Or when one's current self is different then one's image of the ought self one can experience anxiety, fear, pain, and discomfort. A division of current, ideal, and ought self is common among non-binary gender, especially when one first realizes that there is gender discomfort. One may feel identify in one gender manner, though have a different gender ideal. Or one may feel they ought to be a certain gender way, based off of social agent pressures and expectations.

1.3.4 True and False Selves

Sometimes one feels as though they are living a lie, even gender identity wise. The satisfying rewards for performing fake gender behavior lessens and shrinks. The pressures, pain, apathy, discomfort, and confusion of suppressing true behavior, desires, experiences, and urges increases. One receives very little self-esteem from living a false life and nurturing one's false self including gender and gender roles. To a point, everyone has some sort of false self, though when that false self becomes one's primary self, and that which one *is* day-to-day almost every day, then the price of such living can be horrendous.

1.3.5 Cognitive dissonance

When conflicting gender and gender identity beliefs, attitudes, or behavior arise within a non-binary gender person one can either change that cognitive belief, attitude, or behavior, or one can use defense mechanisms to rationalize or justify the conflicts. Non-binary gender persons are more likely to rationalize and justify against non-binary gender, and inhibit behavior and external attitudes at an early age depending on one's gender self esteem, social acceptance, and non-binary gender identity acceptance. Until one seriously confronts goes through the process of gender identity acceptance and understanding, do many untangle the web of deceit, suppression, dissonance, and discrepancies. A period of time where one may uncover that true non-binary gender self. One may be included as of the "other" genders. The process of learning and becoming gendered can be described in terms of nature and nurture.

1.4 Nature and nurture

Our experiences that form our lives and gender identity are molded through a process of *nature* and *nurture*. Nature is the biology that we inherit and develop in the womb, and influence us during our lives. Nurture is the obtained through our interaction with others, beginning with our families, then branching out to those outside the family.

Currently, the medical community has no information concerning non-binary biological development. The closest gender related is a the study of transsexuals *Male-to-Female Transsexuals Have Female Neuron Numbers in a Limbic Nucleus* (Frank P. M. Kruijver, Jiang-Ning Zhou, Chris W. Pool, Michel A. Hofman, Louis J. G. Gooren and Dick F. Swaab). However, no correlation can be made with this study without further experimentation with non-binary persons and comparing the results.

The author does not know of any bran disection, x-ray, CT, PET, MRI, DOI, EROS, EEG, MEG, SPECT, or DNA studies concerning any of the non-binary gender persons.

Summary
Having introduce initial awareness of non-binary gender, the benefits of gender, some basic concepts concerning gender, and some psycho-social-biological issues, we can now turn to trying to learn a little about the group of people that are non-binary. The primary source of this information will be existing polls and surveys already existing in the internet in various non-binary groups, forums, and websites. Sources are cited in the back of the book.

Evidence for non-binary gender for even transsexuals xlx

- On a scale of 1 to 5 (1 is very feminine, 5 is very masculine), where are you on the feminine/masculine spectrum?

FTM, 1 (very feminine for a guy) 0 (0%)

MTF, 1 (very feminine)7 (17.9%)

FTM, 2 (somewhat feminine for a guy) 3 (7.7%)

MTF, 2 (somewhat feminine) 12 (30.8%)

FTM, 3 (neither feminine nor masculine, or androgynous, or whatever...) 2 (5.1%)

MTF, 3 (neither feminine nor masculine, or androgynous, or whatever...) 3 (7.7%)

FTM, 4 (somewhat masculine) 4 (10.3%)

MTF, 4 (somewhat masculine for a girl) 2 (5.1%)

FTM, 5 (very masculine) 5 (12.8%)

MTF, 5 (very masculine for a girl) 0 (0%)

Other (please explain with a comment) 1 (2.6%)

This is based on how masculine or feminine you feel, or how masculine or feminine you want to be, not how you physically look at the moment.

1.5 Wait! Where is the this-is-not-that section?

This is the section, following the basic concepts section, most transgender books, websites, articles, and media starts to tell you what is and is not this-and-that. Sex is not gender. Crossdressers are not transsexuals. Transsexuals are not drag queens or shemales. Androgynes are not androgynous. Genderqueer and androgyne are not the same things.Most crossdressers are not gay. Etc etc etc. But stop....please!"Why?" I ask!

What does this prove or help? I tell you one thing. It can cause more harm then help. The first Gay Transsexual that comes along, can instantly be cast out and hurt. Someone whose sex and gender finally are similar, can be shunned. A Gay crossdresser might not ever mingle with a hetero crossdresser. Androgynous Androgynes might feel as though only their expressions are judged. In other words the first time that two different things combine, human nature and the need to divide tends to cast them aside, except for a few exceptions.

Any transgender persons reading this should recognize this truth. Although the intention might be to help differentiate different aspects of life, such thinking can discriminate lives when applied to judging others.

Any non-trans person can apply such logic to other groups, communities, or organizations.

So instead of filling this space of things non-binary is and is not, I choose to fill it with the reason why I feel such division is harmful, unjust, faulty, and just plain wrong.

And plead with you to please be open to people's individualities. And be ready for seemingly endless mixed identities and persons.

Basic Characteristics found in several polls concerning Non-Binary: Age, Birth Sex, Body Alterations, Gender Expression and Presentation, Orientation, Sexual Preference, Sex/Gender, State of Coming Out

When I was first learning about androgynes, genderqueer, non-binary gender variants the inquisitive nature in me wanted knowledge concerning others, of those things similar and different then me. I began to take polls with a few others in my group and came across similar polls in other groups, concerning different aspects of non-binary gender. The purpose at the time was to find a personal relationship with others, and to see how they felt about different aspects. In this volume, such a list of characteristics can be used to introduce to others those aspects and differences of non-binary gender, sometimes important, other times more trivial. And seldom are these aspects are talked about in any society today.

Note concerning the use of Androgyne and Genderqueer for Non-Binary Gender Variants

*By far, "**androgyne**" is the most common phrase for surveys and polls concerning non-binary gender. Most of the polls contained in this book and on the Internet are titled such. As evidence of the polls that break down the types of Androgynes contained in the groups as well, such connection to the other non-binary genders can be made. I will use in this writing "Androgyne" most of the time to also mean non-binary gender, as well as some uses of "**genderqueer**".*

Note concerning accuracy and sample sizes.

One goal of this book is to try to predict how many non-binary gendered persons are in the US (and possibly the world or other countries). And also to try to judge the accuracy of current data and surveys. Chapter 3 tries to predict the total population. Chapter 2 breaks down that population into characteristics. Chapter 4 subdivides the population into smaller subgroups. All of the tables have ratings of estimated accuracy based on the Chapter 3 population data. And such accuracy rating of all the data is limited to the accuracy of that population prediction, meaning a decrease or increase in population can improve or weaken accuracy of the data, in addition to the normal sample error.

Chapter 2.1 How old are non-binary gender persons?

Developmental psychology may look at age as a measure of certain behavior, and how age affects that behavior throughout one's lifetime. I asked this question "how old are non-binary gender persons" to see whether non-binary gender was specific to an age group or spread broadly and diverse. Three main observations come from the resulting data.

Poll A

Androgyne Age Range[i]

Question How old are you? I am curious as to the androgyne age range.
:

14 - 17	14 (13.5%)
18 - 21	25 (24%)
22 - 26	23 (22.1%)
27 - 30	5 (4.8%)
31 - 34	8 (7.7%)
35 - 39	4 (3.8%)
40 - 44	4 (3.8%)
45 - 49	8 (7.7%)
50 - 54	4 (3.8%)
55 - 59	5 (4.8%)
60 - 64	4 (3.8%)
65 - 70	0 (0%)
70+	0 (0%)

95% confidence +/- 10%

104 non-binaries replied to this poll.

Lack of 65+

I don't think that just because there are no 65+ year old non-binary on this poll, that this means they will die before then. I think it is more a technology hindrance issue. In other words 65+ year olds are less likely to be online to take such polls.

Steady Range

The other age ranges are rather steady from age 14 up to 54 minus the 18 to 26 age group. Considering mortality rates and retirement issues, as well as technology hindrance, one could imagine why the number drops off at around the age of 54.

College Age Group

One can see from the data that the college level age range 18 to 26 is the highest in the amount of non-binary.

The reason for the large number, three times more than other age groups, of 18 to 26 is unknown to the author. Though one can make a number of guesses. This is the college years where people spend most of their time in the academic field. One researches and is involved with others, sometimes exploring one's identity for the first time.

Many people in this age can be full time students, surviving on loans and scholarships, without employment. They can spend more time online and active in such online forums.

Another possibility could be that non-binary gender is just a phase for some.

Further Research
More research could help clarify the reasons for the large group by studying non-binary available time in and out of school, time spent online, and such other reasons. Or try to find former non-binaries that felt as though they just went through a phase.

Also more research can find out why there are no 65+, and if such exist. One can research technology and retirement as possible explanations. Or whether being non-binary gender can lead to early death.

This poll is definitely lacking younger children information for obvious reasons. Child research psychologists can explore such possibilities and areas which are beyond this books limits.

2.2 What biological sex are non-binaries?

The first area after age group one can study is biology. Psychology looks at biology and neuroscience for possible answers concerning influences on behavior.

Biology can influence DNA that influences genetic strengths and weaknesses. DNA has only recently been a focus of science and to my knowledge no known non-binary study has been attempted.

Some TS and Homosexuality studies have been done on the hypothalamus, neurons, and hormones at various stages which show some possible influence, however there is no similar study the author knows of for non-binary gender. One can only make hypothesis from these studies, suggesting that non-binaries may be in between, though no evidence can refute or support such claim at the moment that I know of.

A fundamental question: biological sex
One can start with a fundamental comparison of what percentage of male, female, and intersex body non-binary gender persons there is. While this does no seek to find a cause as the other methods may or may not discover (if there is such biological cause), one can use the evidence to question differences and similarities, especially compared to whole entire populations. And finding such ratios or at least evidence for such ratio, is within my ability.

One can also start to question how if there might be biological influences from the results and hypothesize the possibilities. For instance, crossdressing and transvestism is normally recognize as a mostly male occurrence. Leading one to question why there is very few female crossdressers. Thus making the causes more societal, probably based on lack of tolerance of male populations dressing and expressing femininity.

The question "what biological sex are non-binaries?" is important to see if the non-binary genders are primarily one or how it is spread out among the biological sexes. The I create a pie chart of the average sex body percentage from several sources, though note that such chart is insufficient for entire population use, because of correlation concerns. I consider the pie chart a best guess with reason, rather than being representative with confidence.

We start however with the polls and the raw data summarized on a table and then note observations. Then discuss the correlation issue revealing different polls as we go.

The Data

This data covers eight polls that contains data concerning the biology of non-binary gender the first 7 came from androgyne websites. The last one came from a genderqueer website.

Sex	Poll B	Poll C	Poll D	Poll F	App A	App B	App D	LiveJournal Poll	Totals-Avg*	
Intersex	1	0	2	2	2	0	X	0	7	1.0
Female	9	3	12	18	0	4	7	29	82	10.25
Male	17	22	57	21	10	12	35	5	179	22.38
Totals	27	25	71	41	12	16	42	34	268	

Total results and averages are expected to produce 95% confidence +/-6% when considering 268 total samples.

Irregularities in the polls
Looking at the data Poll C and App A are the most irregular. Poll C compared to the other 5, should statistically have 1 intersexed. App A should have 2 to 4 females. It is unknown why these two polls have these differences, compared to the other 5 which are somewhat similar. The LiveJournal genderqueer poll has many more female born non-binary versus male born non-binary gender. Such poll is evidence of female born accepting the label of genderqueer, and sometimes preferring it.

There is a sharp divide between the percentage of biological makeup of the polls from the androgyne poll sources and the genderqueer poll. The non-binary community may be headed towards a separation of genderqueer and androgyne identities based off of birth assigned sex, though still there are some that identify as both. For now, gender identity wise, those that identify as either have essential the same overall general issues, though possibly different basis and perceptions, as well as different smaller details inherent in one's birth sex .

Intersex Bodied Non-Binary
The **average 2.68%** of non-binary are intersex bodied. The polls do not differentiate being born intersex and using hormones and surgeries to create mixed sexual characteristics, however true intersex medical condition is assumed.
*The percentages of the individual polls that have intersex are: Poll D 2.8%, Poll B 3.7%, Poll F 4.88%, App A 16.67%. So a regular range of **between 3% and 5%** of*

28

non-binary are Intersex bodied, minus the abnormal 16.67% of App A.

One of the major questions that enters the mind after reading this data is, "why is there a lack of greater number intersex non-binary population?" If the statistics for intersex is correct and at first glance, non-binary gender would seem to go well with naturally born intersex. After all, intersex are born with mixed biology, and non-binary gender accepts and seeks mixed or neither gender. One special note is the disconnect that intersex emphasizes sometimes from the transgender community. Intersex are not transgender. Or that there is a much higher preference of becoming "normal". Further research into this area could prompt answers. As well as answer such questions as: How do many intersex feel about, evaluate the ideas, and judge the behavior of non-binary gender identities? And further research might go towards birth intersex that do identify as non-binary.

Female Bodied Non-Binary
The **average 30.59%** of non-binary are female bodied.

The percentages of the individual polls that have females are: Poll C 12%, App D 16.67%, Poll D 16.90%, App B 25%, Poll B 33.33%, Poll F 43.90%, irregular LJ poll 85.29%.
So a regular range of between 12% and 44% of non-binary are Female bodied.

One question one can ask is, "why is the female birth body percentage under half of the total of male birth body percentage?" This despite the world's population being slightly higher for females. This may also be similar to the TS differences between male and female born body persons. Or is this related to a technology gap, and there really are more female born non-binary. Or is this just because 7 of the surveys are androgyne which is male born dominant, versus 1 genderqueer from which if we had 7 surveys (which though I looked and continue to look for more, I can't find anymore) it would be more realistic number?

Male Bodied Non-Binary
The **average of 66.79%** of non-binary are male bodied.

The percentages of the individual polls that have males are: irregular LJ Poll 14.71%, Poll F 51.22% Poll B 62.96% App B 75% Poll D 80.28% App A 83.33% App D 83.33% Poll C 88%. So a regular range of between 51% and 88% of non-binary are Male bodied.

- Male Bodied
- Female Bodied
- Inter-sexed Bodied

Statistical Correlation of male to female bodied non-binary gender

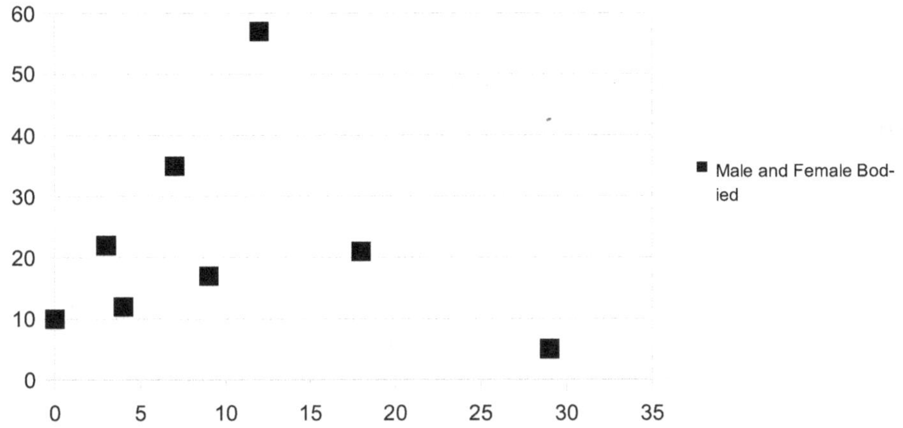

Axis
X is female bodied
Y is male bodied

Number of Observations=	8

Female Bodied

Mean and Standard Deviation =	10.25 +/-9.44

Male Bodied

Mean and Standard Deviation =	22.38 +/-16.70
Linear Regression y-intercept =	24.28
Linear Regression slope =	-0.19
Correlation Coefficient =	-0.10

Notes Concerning the correlation of the data
The -0.10 raw data correlation coefficient shows only slight negative correlation of male bodied to female bodied, though it fails to correlate sufficiently. The closer to -1 (or +1 if it was negative, 0 is no correlation) the more the two bodied sexes correlate for the sample

sizes, compared to a possible population.

The .10 can be used to find the percentage of common linear correlation by the formula 0.10*0.10=0.01 *100= 1%. 99% is not common. Imagine two circles overlapping 1%. That area would be how much these two bodied gender information correlates between the percentage of male bodied and female bodied for to develop a ratio, along a linear slope.

The biggest problem is from the irregular polls. However scientifically one must present the data truthfully. So this correlation shows that the pie chart ratio division that I included is very much unreliable, rather it is only a best guess. The the correlation of the data fails by a great amount. More surveys from different sources may increase the reliability of the data someday. Or someone taking a massive survey may find a more accurate ratio of birth sex for non-binary gender.

One good question that this lack of correlation creates is, "why doesn't the data correlate?"

Poll B
Are you male-bodied or female-bodied? [ii]
Are you male-bodied or female-bodied?

I am male-bodied.	17 (63%)
I am female-bodied.	9 (33.3%)
I am intersexed.	1 (3.7%)

This chart shows a ratio of I:F:M of 1:9:17

Poll C
Question
What is your sex? (tick the one that best applies to you)[iii]
Responses

Choices	Votes
I was born female but have acquired some male features	1
I am transitioning from male to female	3
I am transitioning from female to male	0
I was born female	2
I was born intersexed (diagnosed)	0
I was born male	7
I was born male but my body shows some female features	8
I was born female but my body shows some male features	0
I was born male but have acquired some female features	4

This chart shows a ratio of F:M of 3:22. I will talk more about this poll next section concerning non-binary transitions.

What is your sex and gender?[iv]

Poll D

Question

What is your sex and gender?

Responses

Votes

Choices

Choices	Votes
Male-born man	3
Female-born woman	0
Male-born androgyne	45
Female-born androgyne	10
Male-born woman	9
Female-born man	2
Intersex-born androgyne	1
Intersex-born man	0
Intersex-born woman	1
Other	7

This poll is more like the sex mixes birth sex and gender from the same forum as the prior post. This post seems more in line with the results of the first post. This says I:F:M non-binary ratio of **2:12:57.**

2.3 How do non-binaries change or desire to change their bodies?

A comparison of birth body versus transition, organized by size of sample.

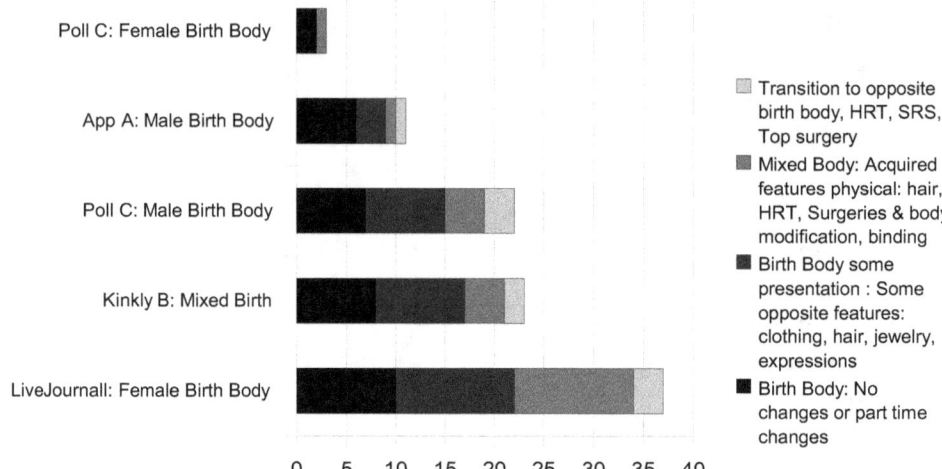

I created this chart to visually see how the birth bodies are or will be affected by one's non-binary gender identity and to see how consistent, accurate, and reliable the various source information might be.

Some Assumptions I have made in the chart above

Some sources I "fill in gaps" for comparison which might create some inaccuracies, in order make assumptions about things other sources leave out. The biggest assumption I make is that those that desire something will eventually get it someway. For example: in Kinkly's B poll I used the "I show both male & female physical characteristics" in the acquired features: hair, HRT, Surgeries & body modification, binding. I decided to do this not based off of the current status of those that commented on this connection, rather also on the prior poll called Kinkly A, where they express the desire to change the body to "show male and female parts." I do so under the assumption that they will indeed achieve such desire either through a therapist or DIY HRT, and/or possibly achieve some cosmetic surgery. And that hair cut and/or hair removal might be part of such transition and presentation. Binding and/or breast removal might be in the future of some. So my assumption is that they will get what they desire, if they haven't already. An error might arise if there are any that wish to show both male and female physical characteristics that doesn't include the desire for HRT, surgeries (various), body modification, hair removal, or binding.

Poll C I had to try deciding what "shows some" opposite sex features and what "acquired some" opposite sex features meant compared to the other options of "transitioning" to opposite sex and just plain being born that way with no stated transition or opposite features. In this case I take "acquired" to mean something major or significant, such as HRT, binding, surgery, hair, earrings and such.

App A I had to try figuring out what "body not completely conform to birth sex" meant, and I put it also under the acquired/show male and female section. I considered "body not at all conform to birth sex" and "transitioning to the other sex" because they were the same voting results, and seemed logically the same if not nearly the same.

Focus of this analysis
The major focus of this series is to see how biological sex is or might be altered or not altered. I have 2 sources of information for both male and female born bodied non-binary, and one mixed source. As one looks at the break down, one can see that which body a person is born in does not have much of an influence on the percentage of non-binary body modification and expression.

From this evidence I can make the hypothesis one additional statement that *birth gender has very little relationship towards the percentage of non-binary body modification and transitioning.In other words male born non-binaries are not more inclined to change their bodies over female born non-binaries.*

*Lack of **Intersex bodied** information*
There is however no Intersex bodied information organized anywhere that I could find, except mixed with other non-binary persons. App A would show some data if there was a way to know how the 2 intersex that voted picked the other choices. This is one issue someone should address at a future time.

2.3.1 Female Bodied
The only Female bodied information from one poll C is that 1 out of 3 (33.33%) females have acquired some male features.

The main poll that I have found data concerning female bodied transitions is from LiveJournal[v]. Additional female bodied information can be gathered from this source. Most members on this genderqueer LiveJournal site identify as genderqueer over androgyne.

2.3.1.1 Female birth bodied hormones and surgeries   33

Of the female bodied responders, 10 out of 29 (34.48%) don't have any transition plans at the moment. 12 out of 29 (41.38%) had "other" plans. 6 out of 29 (20.69%) are on hormones, with half of those (3 females born, 10.34%) post-op ftm, while the others (non-op) have no plans for surgery.

One question one can look into is, "What are the "other"plans?" Is it clothing, binding, and hair related? The only facts known is that it doesn't include hormones nor surgery.

2.3.2   *Male Bodied*
2.3.2.1 Female vs Male Features
The Male data however is sufficient from poll C. 8 of 22 (36%) of males were born male but shows some female features. Also 4 out of 22 (18%) have acquired some female features. And 3 out of 22 (14%) of males are transitioning from male to female. 7 out of 22 (31%) of males are just male, without female influence.

Most likely meaning out of male born Androgynes: 31% are male bodied, 36% have feminine appearance influences (hair, jewelry, makeup, clothing), 18% have "acquired" major changes mainly HRT, and 14% are headed towards full transtion and SRS or gender nullification.

2.3.3 How do non-binary gender persons want (desire) to change or have changed their bodies?(mixed birth body data)
Of those that chose to change their bodies, or desire to do so, how would or are they changing them. Add to these prior two sources a newer third poll from Kinkly (Kinkly A) which asked a few months ago if androgynes feel the need to change their bodies and what ways. Clearly there is a split between showing both, being neutral, neither, or other. Out of 29 answers.
Kinkly A

:		
yes I wish to show both male & fem parts		10 (34.5%)
yes a more neutral look		8 (27.6%)
yes i want to show no gendered parts		4 (13.8%)
yes other		4 (13.8%)
yes but not for gender reasons		2 (6.9%)
no I'd be happy in any body		1 (3.4%)
no my body is androgynic already		0 (0%) 34
no other		0 (0%)

A third of Androgynes desire both parts. Another third desires neutrality of their bodies. A few desire no gender parts or other changes. The "other" may contain the 6% to 14% desiring full transition to opposite sex of birth sex (based off of the other polls). Only one Androgyne was happy in current or any body, which is similar to the low percentage of Androgynes, 2 out of 16 (12.5%) , not desiring any androgynous or transitional traits.

This poll shows definitely a desire of Androgynes to change their bodies, in slightly different ways. These different focuses of changes (both, neither, none, other) may correspond to the subgroups of Androgynes mentioned in a chapter 4, as well as the state or goals of one's transition mentioned before. And such variety of transitioning between non-binaries leads to the one of the main issues of Androgynes mentioned in that chapter of obstacles and issues of Androgynes of no set paths, individual nature of Androgynes, as well as one having ongoing transitions.

Despite having mentioned these obstacles, a few common transition patterns can be seen from the data. And this data may help others looking for information on how others feel concerning transitioning as an Androgyne.

2.3.4 App A: mostly male birth (though 2 intersex)
Those that answered the polls 50% (6 out of 12) have bodies that conform to their birth sex. Of those non-binary that answered 25% (3 out of 12) are taking hormones (HRT) and may or may not be the same as the 25% (3 out of 12) whose body does not completely confirm to birth sex. 8.33% (1 out of 12) says that their body does not conform at all to their birth sex, and 8.33% (1 out of 12) is transitioning to the other sex. These last two may or may not be the same person.

2.3.5 App B: mixed M and F
Although there is a lot of data on this survey, most of the data deals with birth sex, presentation, religion, and sexuality. There is one piece of data however that 6.25% (1 out of 16) is transitioning to the other sex.

35

2.3.6 A comparison of desired HRT and Sex Change language various sources

Poll / Survey	HRT	Sex Change
Poll C: female birth	33.33%?("acquired")	?
Poll C: male birth	18%? ("acquired")	14% (are transitioning)
LiveJournal: female birth	20.69% (HRT)	10.34% (post-op)
Kinkly A: mixed birth	34.5%?("desire show mixed parts")	13.8%? ("yes other", no sex change option in poll)
App A: male/intersex birth	25% (HRT)("body not completely conform to birth")	8.33% ("transitioning to other sex")=("body does not at all conform to birth")?
App B: mixed birth	?	6.25% (transitioning to other sex)

? = unknown. Some key words are included to cite evidence.

From these various sources, it appears to me that about 20%-25% of non-binaries are taking hormones, one way or another, based off of the LiveJournal & App A numbers which are specific. 10% getting SRS type major operations, based off of the post-op LiveJournal results. I assume all of the post-ops have taken hormones. Another 5% appears to be transitioning, based off of the other higher results. Though some of the results from the LiveJournal poll present as opposite birth gender, without taking hormones or getting SRS.

The other 10%-20% that are taking hormones with or without other alterations, I assume remain in an in-between sex state, altered by the effects of the hormones.

Another 10% to 15% alter their bodies in other major ways such as surgeries, hair removal (electrolysis + laser), binding, and major hair changes (hair cuts, styling, color). This additional amount may or may not account for the higher, non-HRT specific answers "body not completely conform to birth", "desire to show mixed parts", and "acquired features.

2.3.7 Progression and Depth of Transitioning
There are 2 other polls with supporting or additional data concerning Male bodied non-binary transitioning App A and App B. Especially the

portion of the poll at App B is very informative since it shows a progression of depth of transitioning.

From Poll at

App B

Looking androgynous is not my thing	2
Part-time androgyny suits me well	2
I would like to be a full-time androgyne but cannot	4
I intend to become a full-time androgyne	1
I am (or becoming) a full-time androgyne	9
I am transitioning to be the other sex	1

16 sample size has 90% confidence with +/-20.5%

From Poll at App A

If a magic wand could change my sex, I would do it	9
If men could wear whatever they want, I would have very few gender problems left	7
My body conforms to my birth sex	6
My body does not completely conform to my birth sex	3
My body does not conform at all to my birth sex	1
I have been mistaken as the other sex (related to birth sex)	4
I am transitioning to the other sex	1
I have taken hormones	3
I have seriously comtemplated with the idea of changing my sex	4
More than 50% of time, I wear items that are usually only worn by the other sex	10

12 sample size has a 90% confidence with +/-24%

2.4-2.9 Non-Binary Transitions: Roles, Expressions, & Presentation

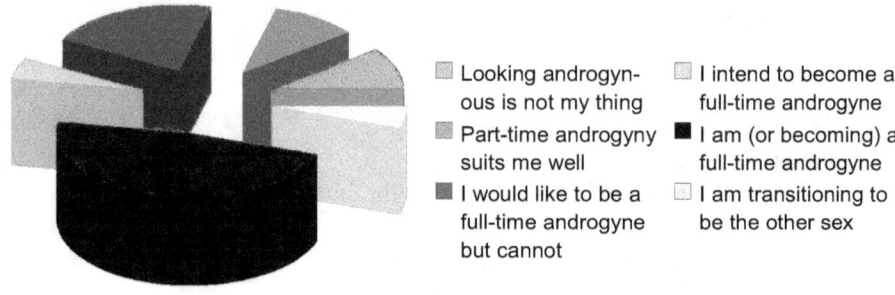

Looking androgyn-
ous is not my thing

Part-time androgyny
suits me well

I would like to be a
full-time androgyne
but cannot

I intend to become a
full-time androgyne

I am (or becoming) a
full-time androgyne

I am transitioning to
be the other sex

2.4 App B: Mixed Birth Body Poll
2.4.1 Birth Presentation
These male bodied are probably split between those just fine with their bodies and appearance and those that are part-time androgynous.

Non-Binary that are fine as they are
And from App B only 2 out of 16 (**12.5%**) as not having looking androgynous as a goal.

2.4.2 Androgynous
2.4.2.1 Part-time Androgyny
As for looking androgynous 2 out of 16 (**12.5%**) are fine with part time androgyny. I assume this is appearance wise meaning clothing, hair (style, cut, or wigs), jewelry, binding, temporary hair removal, and makeup or such.

2.4.2.2 Would like to be a full-time androgynous but cannot
Of those that answered 4 out of 16 (**25%**) would like to be full-time androgynous but cannot. There are many barriers to such presenting androgynous and coming out, many of which will be presented in the non-binary issues and unequal rights section.

2.4.2.3 Androgynous Non-Binary(full-time)
Of those that answered 9 out of 16 (**56.25%**) are presenting themselves as androgynous non-binary full-time. And 1 out of 16 (6.25%) intends to become a full-time non-binary. Chapter 4, Polls A and B shows the great influence of non-binary gender identity on androgynous presentation.

Poll A shows about 50% of non-binary's appearance being influenced by their non-binary gender. Poll B shows clothing only second to interests as being greatly different from one's birth gender, followed by hair, accessories, and makeup.

2.4.3 SRS
Androgynes full transitioning
Poll App B, 1 out of 16 (6.25%) are transitioning to the other sex.

2.5App A
From the poll in App A 7 of 10 (70%)male bodied answered that "If men could wear whatever they want, I would have very few gender problems left." And 10 of 12 (83%) said that "More than 50% of time, I wear items that are usually only worn by the other sex."
1 out of 12 (8.33%) has desires to transition to the opposite of one's birth sex.

2.6 LiveJournal
2.6.1 Female Bodied Gender Role
When asked what gender role they were currently living in, there were several different responses.

2.6.2 *Different Genders* at different times- 10 out of the 29 (34.48%) present themselves as different genders at different times. Either as fluid or part time androgynous roles.

2.6.3 *Neither Gender*- 6 out of 29 (20.69%) have said that they present themselves as neither gender role.

2.6.4 *Androgyne*- 4 out of 29 (13.79%) have said that they present themselves as androgynes, maybe meaning both or neither gender, or androgynously roles.

2.6.5 *Male*- 5 of the 29 (17.24%) presents themselves as male gender roles.

2.6.6 *Female*- Only 5 out of the 29 (17.24%) present themselves as female gender roles.

2.7 Poll: Kinkly B

Question: How do you present yourself in public

as your birth gender
6 (22.2%)
I wear androgynous clothing from other side but still look like birth gender
4 (14.8%)
I show both male & female physical characteristics
4 (14.8%)
changes depending on how I feel from day to day
4 (14.8%)
wear clothing from both sides
3 (11.1%)
as the opposite of birth gender
2 (7.4%)
I show no clealy Male/Female trait
2 (7.4%)
other
2 (7.4%)

Total Members Voted: 27

This poll focuses on presentation (gender expression) to the public, probably meaning in everyday live, beyond the confines of the home. It concerns those outward image type elements. It does not show the degree of such presentation, nor the specifics, though some comment on how they present in the comments following the poll.

How one presents themselves in the home and exclusively online, are not the focus of this study. There is a great degree of being "out" assumed in this survey, towards at least some people, if one reviews the coming out survey (Poll I), most likely one's partner, best friends, and possibly a few strangers. Though fewer are out at work, so employment and classrooms may force many to not present such manner according to Poll I.

2.8 Are non-binary persons happy with their presentation?
Kinkly did another poll to find out this answer. Although one may present in one manner, one may truly desire to present in a much different manner. A

discrepancy in one's actual self and ones ideal self might exist which prevents happiness and may cause sadness and disappointment. A discrepancy can occur between one's actual self and ought self may cause great internal agony, pain, fear, and anxiety. Much of the answer has to do with what type of presentation one is currently presenting.

The most happiness comes from non-binary and opposite birth gender presentation.

Kinkly C: Poll

Question: are you happy with your presentation

Birth Gender Presentation

I present as my birth gender and thats good
1 (4%)

I present as my birth gender and its a compromise
6 (24%)

I present as my birth gender and thats not good
2 (8%)

Non-Binary Presentation

I present in a non binary way and it's good
7 (28%)

I present in a non binary way and it's a compromise
2 (8%)

I present in a non binary way and it's not good
0 (0%)

Opposite Birth Gender Presentation

I present as the opposite of my birth gender and thats good
4 (16%)

I present as the opposite of my birth gender and its a compromise
0 (0%)

I present as the opposite of my birth gender and thats not good
0 (0%)

Other Presentation

other good
0 (0%)

other bad
0 (0%)

other compromise
3 (12%)

Total Members Voted: 25

41

Although this number is small, the amount of Androgynes having considered SRS is relatively high. 4 out of 12 (25%) of App B seriously considered sex change. Also as mentioned in the Preface, 15 of 40 (37.5%) expressed their serious extreme discomfort with one's birth gender and considered SRS or HRT. In that same poll another 14 out of 40 (35%) expressed that their gender discomfort "changes, sometimes intense, sometimes not".

So 25% to 37.5% of Androgynes have considered SRS, though 6% to 14% actually transition, though the other 25% does HRT without transition.

This other 25% can experience changes in the physical body creating an androgynous intersex-like sexual anatomy in a few ways as the next section shows with both, neutral, neither, or other. And these 25% are probably more likely members of the sndrogynous non-binaries (full-time).

Androgynes and breasts poll xlix

- As a female-born androgyne:

I'm comfortable with my breasts (1 votes [3.12%]) Percentage of vote: 3.12%

I'm not comfortable with my breasts but wouldn't seek top surgery (8 votes [25.00%]) Percentage of vote: 25.00%

I'm seeking or have acquired top surgery (5 votes [15.62%]) Percentage of vote: 15.62%

N/A - I'm a male-born androgyne (18 votes [56.25%]) Percentage of vote: 56.25%

- As a male-born androgyne:

I'm comfortable with my chest (1 votes [3.12%]) Percentage of vote: 3.12%

I'm not comfortable with my chest but wouldn't seek breast growth/augmentation (6 votes [18.75%]) Percentage of vote: 18.75%

I'm seeking or have acquired breast growth/augmentation (11 votes [34.38%]) Percentage of vote: 34.38%

N/A - I'm a female-born androgyne (14 votes [43.75%])

2.9 Details of presentations, one can find more information from a poll I did long ago.

What parts of your grooming or your body (maintaining or changing) interests you as an androgyne (you can vote more than one)?

Hair (on head) http://www.susans.org/forums/index.php/topic,9549.0.html
25 (9.6%)

Body Hair http://www.susans.org/forums/index.php/topic,9357.0.html
25 (9.6%)

Weight, Proportion, vs Height - Body Shape
http://www.susans.org/forums/index.php/topic,11550.msg84124.html#msg84124
25 (9.6%)

Scent, odor, perfume, cologne
http://www.susans.org/forums/index.php/topic,13790.0.html
9 (3.5%)

Earrings, or other body piercings
12 (4.6%)

Tattoos http://www.susans.org/forums/index.php/topic,13535.0.html
8 (3.1%)

Eyebrows- shape
16 (6.2%)

Facial use of Makeup- Androgyne Techniques, or feminine techniques
13 (5%)

Clothing styles- Androgyne styles
http://www.susans.org/forums/index.php/topic,9779.0.html
24 (9.2%)

Clothing colors- http://www.susans.org/forums/index.php/topic,9779.0.html
20 (7.7%)
http://www.susans.org/forums/index.php/topic,12443.0.html

Finger nails- Length, color, strength
15 (5.8%)

Wearing Jewelry-
10 (3.8%)

Chest - Flat (hiding any sort of breast-like shape, or removal)
8 (3.1%)

Chest- Breasts (having some sort of breasts - Real or synthetic)
19 (7.3%)   43

Skin -color, moisture, condition, clearity
11 (4.2%)

Voice- Sound, vocabulary

Breasts
By far *breasts, or lack thereof* are the number one interest of non-binary gender. The point of view of the subject depends mostly on one's birth sex. And from such a point of view one may wish to either diminish, reduce, and remove or enlarge, emphasize, and create breasts.

Hair
Hair is tied for next popular emphasis. Hair has been called the window frame to the face, which frames the eyes, the windows to the soul. Hair can reflect one's personality, as well as emphasize or deemphasis one's facial structure, helping to shape one's facial structure.

Length as well as cut can feminize, neutralize, or masculinize one's appearance.

Style, wave/straight, patterns/braids/ponytails can also alter one's appearance. Color and highlights can also be altered.

Baldness and hair loss can create challenges for male born non-binary.

Clothing
Clothing is tied for hair for emphasis of non-binary persons. Clothing along with the other style elements of appearance, can reflect one's inner self. One's outer image communicates to others certain messages. It can also be functional, with pockets, symbols of status, uniforms

Body Shape
Ones body shape can limit or emphasis the types of clothing one may wear. Besides affecting the dimensions of the clothing, certain styles are limited to certain sizes. One's actual body shape may require certain style rules, if one is to minimize certain prominent features and emphasize important strengths. One may be able to alter one's body shape through several methods.

44

Body Hair
Removal of body hair can bring some relief to male born non-binaries.
Either temporary methods such as shaving, sugar/wax, depilatory, tweezing,
or bleaching can be used. Or permanent methods can be sought out such as
laser and electrolysis hair removal. Some hrt removes or decreases body hair.

The addition of body hair in female born non-binaries is mainly through hrt.
Though stage style adhesive facial and body hair can be used also.

Clothing Styles
If you look in department and clothing stores, or online at clothing websites,
clothing normally is divided into men, boys, women, girls sections. The styles
within these these sections vary greatly. How these fit on the body may also
vary greatly. Sizing differs and conversions normally are needed. Material also
Differs. Masculine material can be more rugged. Feminine lighter, silkier,
softer, and lacier. A play on cuts can bring results. There are neutral cuts also.

Clothing Colors
Colors themselves have meanings. Pink, yellows, and pastels for girls and
blues, neutrals, and dark colors for boys seems all too common in one's
infancy. A play with color can bring dramatic results. Neutral colors can be
non-gendered.

Eyebrows
One can shape and sculpt eyebrows to feminize or masculinize eyebrows. Thin
arched eyebrows more feminine.

Fingernails
Fingernails can be grown out, shaped, shortened, and polish added in various
color or clear coated. Acrylics and gel nails can be used to extend nails.

Makeup or lack of it
Makeup can be used to cover flaws, enhance features, and create styles, or not
used to create a more natural look.

Earrings and piercings
Ears and other body parts can ad various body jewelry to accent styles.

2.10 What are the orientations of non-binaries?

Orientation has been a topic of conversation for Androgynes in several posts, websites, and discussions. Nero asked this question using simple terms of attracted to women, attracted to men, bisexual, and asexual. Certainly the language of orientation has expanded to terms such as pansexual, omnisexual, and specific terms to mean what one is attracted to. However these four should be sufficient for a beginning look into Androgyne orientation.

Poll F

Androgyne Orientation[vii]
Question What is your sexual orientation?
:

I am male bodied and attracted to men.	0 (0%)
I am male bodied and attracted to women.	9 (22%)
I am male bodied and bisexual.	11 (26.8%)
I am male bodied and asexual.	1 (2.4%)
I am female bodied and attracted to men.	3 (7.3%)
I am female bodied and attracted to women.	3 (7.3%)
I am female bodied and bisexual.	11 (26.8%)
I am female bodied and asexual.	1 (2.4%)
I am IS and attracted to men.	0 (0%)
I am IS and attracted to women.	1 (2.4%)
I am IS and bisexual.	1 (2.4%)
I am IS and asexual.	0 (0%)

95% confidence at +/-12%

Bisexuality

Bisexuality is very high for Androgynes, according to this poll, with half, 22 out of 41 (53.7%), revealing such preferences. Also when male bodied and female bodied Androgynes populations are near the same, bisexuality is identical.

Stark difference

Interesting to note that although many male born Androgynes claim bisexuality, no males are attracted only to men. Though many male born Androgynes are attracted to females, 9 out of 41 (21.95%). This is very different for female born Androgynes, in which as many attracted to females as men, 3 (7.3% for both).

Asexuality
This poll shows only 2 (4.8%) asexual, though the next one, Poll G, shows more Asexuals
Poll G

Question

Are you Asexual or Sexual?[viii]

Responses

Choices Votes

Asexual androgyne	6	37
Sexual androgyne	10	62

90% confidence at +/-20%

This poll shows 6 of its 16 (37%) responders as being Asexual. Whereas the prior poll only showed 2:41 (4.8%) being Asexual.

What is your gender?

Female	[**31**]	[35.23%]
Male	[**24**]	[27.27%]
Without gender	[**13**]	[14.77%]
Having both male and female gender	[**4**]	[4.55%]
Being somewhere between male and female gender	[**10**]	[11.36%]
Being a gender other than male or female	[**6**]	[6.82%]

Retrieved 6/19/09 from http://www.asexuality.org/en/index.php?showtopic=39551

This poll, taken from the AVEN forum, reveals of asexuals taking this poll 37.5%, about a third, as being something other than male or female gender wise. Also an additional poll on the same page breaks the results down further in that 13.64% positively identify as transgender, where as and additional 13.64% sometimes identify as transgender. Next the results for identifying as genderqueer are, 23.86% positively do so, and an additional 18.18% sometimes identify as one.

2.11 What are the sexual preferences of non-binaries?

The next poll is not very helpful. Without know the percentage of characteristics of the voters, it becomes more a popularity of gender orientation preferences. Though there is one interesting feature based off of the prior post.

Poll H

Question
What is your sexual preference? [ix]

Responses

Choices	Votes
males	29
females	60
male-born androgynes	39
female-born androgynes	49
transmen (FTM)	24
transwomen (MTF)	38
intersexed people	31
you yourself	17
other	15
none of the above	5

95 confidence at +/-12%

Female and MTF preference
Of course females is the highest of all the preferences. Which can be explained by the high bisexuality, high population of male born, and few female born. Interesting to note however is that the preference of MTF however is 22 (36.7%) votes less. So 1 in 3 Androgynes that have female preference to not prefer MTF.

Female-Born Androgynes
Next highest is female-born Androgynes. Almost as high as females,49, 11 (18%) votes less than females, though higher than MTF. Unknown is the reason for the drop. Androgynes do significantly find female-born Androgynes different than females.

Male-Born Androgynes
Male-born Androgynes have the third highest votes, nearly the same as MTF. Opposite of female/female-born Androgyne relationship, the males are preferred 16.7% less than male-born Androgynes.

Intersex Androgynes
Intersex Androgynes are preferred below Androgynes and females. The rarity of Intersex however decreases the likelihood of meeting one.

Males and FTM
Males are preferred near last, besides oneself, along with FTM.

When combining the information of Poll F to H, its interesting to see the similarities and differences between the birth sexes.

From Poll at App B

My sexuality is mainstream	4
I like S&M things (broadly understood)	0
I have sexual fetishes (at least one)	7
I am a sexual voyeur (affects your behavior)	2
I am a sexual exhibitionist (have done it in real life)	2

In addition to sexual preferences of sex/gender of person, there is a poll showing a little more information about sexual activity preferences. This poll is by 10 male-born and 2 intersex born.

*Most Androgynes have at least one sexual fetish, 7 out of 12 (58.33%).
*One third, 4 out of 12 (33.33%) consider themselves sexual mainstream.
*A few are voyeur and exhibitionists 2 out of 12 (16.67%).   49

2.12 What is the non-binary state of coming out?

Next one can analyze the non-binary state of being of out or coming out to others.

How many people know you are non-binary?   x

Poll I

How many people know you are an androgyne? (click all that apply)

No one at the moment.	6 (9.1%)
No one, I just realized I am an androgyne, and havent told anyone yet.	3 (4.5%)
One person	1 (1.5%)
Two people	5 (7.6%)
Three people or more	13 (19.7%)
My family	1 (1.5%)
My best friend	10 (15.2%)
My partner	12 (18.2%)
My coworkers / classmates	1 (1.5%)
Some strangers	4 (6.1%)
I tell everyone	0 (0%)
I dont want to answer this poll	0 (0%)
No one will ever know	1 (1.5%)
The whole community	0 (0%)
I will tell more soon as I can	5 (7.6%)
Therapist / Psychologist / Psychiatrist / Councilor	4 (6.1%)

29 voters at least: 90% confidence at +/- 15%

I think one question that I wish I had asked in this poll is how many only tell online friends.

Non-binaries are having a rough time telling family members and other community members. In other words, their coming out to their best friends and partners okay, but not to their family. Some are even talking to therapists.

About 20% up to 30% have not told anyone.

Partners and best friends seem to be the main targets of non-binary coming out.   50

Poll J

How comfortable you are with your gender identity? [xi]

Question

How comfortable you are with your gender identity?

Responses

Choices	Votes
I am in closet even to myself	0
I am in closet to everyone else	8
I am in closet except to my closest friends	15
I am mostly in closet	7
I am mostly out of closet	9
I vaguely remember there having been a closet	0
My closet - yes, full of nice clothes	3
I am who I am	24
I help people come out from closets	2
I change the gender rules	6

Confidence and error unknown

I don't know the details of this poll. I think the 3 main pieces of information from this poll is that it shows 9 mostly out of the closet. And that 8 are in the closet. And that 15 have only told closest friend. Again this shows the focus of non-binary coming out is best friends and partners. Certainly miles behind the gay and lesbian community.

Rarity and lack of local community structures could be one cause of such isolation, when compared to more "out" communities.

I think interesting that despite this lack of "coming out", expressive non-binary genders have the potential to be "out" by not "passing". Passing for most in the community is not a goal nor desired.

Certainly those that blur gender expression are always out.

Summary

The age, birth sex, body transitions, gender expressions, orientations, and state of coming-out for non-binary genders vary, though there are some common paths within these individualistic lives. Following the chapters on gender, characteristics, and basic issues, a population will be attempted to be found using a few methods.

3 How many non-binaries are there?

Although the answer is not clearly counted anywhere, some mathematics will try to extrapolate a theoretical number for the USA and World. There are many estimate numbers for different transgender persons floating around.

3.1 Transsexual Ratio Method
3.1.1 Transsexual numbers

From Lynn Conway's site, the best TS estimate can be found using data from existing transsexual surgeries performed by major SRS doctors since the beginning. The number of MTF TS is more likely 1:500 to 1:250[xii] compared to traditionally understated numbers. FTM is normally 1 for every 4 of MTF, very similar to the ratio of male-bodied to female-bodied androgynes. So for every 1,000 to 2,000 there is 4 MTF and 1 FTM, equaling 5 transsexuals.

3.1.2 Non-Binary Ratio to Transsexual and its Assumptions

In order to find estimate of non-binaries, I looked at available data from sites that contains transgender persons, and includes TS and non-binaries. One can find a ratio of TS vs non-binary, given many assumptions of course.

1. That the members of the site are in fact what they claim, TS and AG.
2. That the percentage of transsexuals and androgynes represented in the website similar to the population of the country and world.

5 Sources 1.) The population of androgynes at the source website is 146. All of the transsexual populations added up is 848. So with a 146/848 ratio, one can come up with 0.1721 or 17.21%. **2.)** A poll on that same source comes up with a near number of 16.47[xiii]. **3.)** The UMass study, although the survey data cannot be used because of obvious reasons, [xiv] though unclear and probably less accurate due to wording has from the phone interviews 10% androgyne, 51% MTF, 23% FTM, equalling a ratio of 10/74 and androgynes 0.1351 or 13.51% of TS. **4.)** And from the Emails a ratio of 8/68 to equal 0.1176 or 11.76%. **5.)** From the IFGE (see poll bellow) comes a ratio of 85/458 (85 consisting of genderqueers, two spirits, and agender). "I think I need a bigger box" could mean anything in this context I think including crossdressers and more. This leads to a .1886 or 18.86%.

So for every 100 transsexuals is 19, 17, 16, 14, 11 non-binaries. All the ratios from three major sources are consistently close between 11 and 19 percent (all within 8% of each other), averaging **15.56%**. Roughly 1 non-binary for every 6 transsexuals.

3.1.3 Correlating the Data

To check whether the data collected from these 5 different sources, are correlated together, even at different amounts, the correlation and then regression are taken of the 5 data sources.

Number of sources:	*5*
Linear Regression y-intercept	*31.17*
Linear Regression slope	*5.47*
Correlation Coefficient	*0.99*

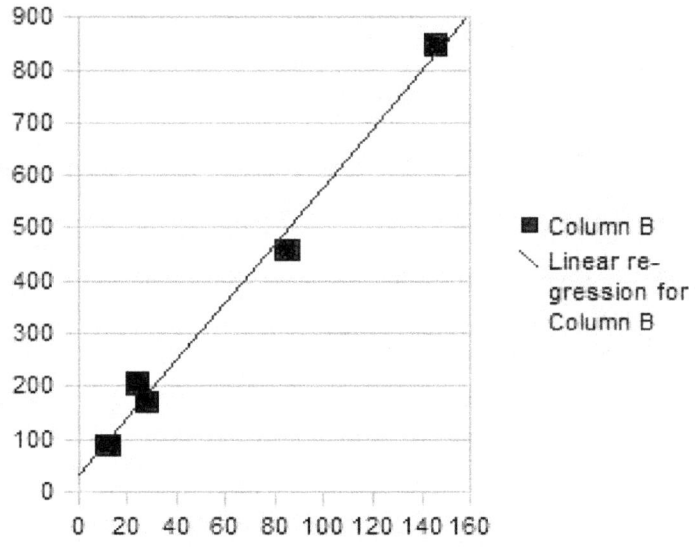

X=Non-Binaries
Y=Transsexuals

Non-Binaries : Transsexuals

146	848
28	171
12	87
24	205
85	458

Data Correlation Passes

The data absolutely passes the correlation as 98% correlation between the non-binary populations and the transsexual populations.

3.1.4 Non-Binary Estimate Prevalence

Armed with the average ratio which is consistent, one can apply it to the Lynn Conway's modern estimate transsexual ratio data, coming up with the answer of **1:1285** to **1:2571 non-binary prevalence**.

3.1.5 Estimate United States Non-Binary Population

Current USA populations as of Sept 7, 2008 as I write this is 305,088,478. Which brings up a number of **118,665** to **237, 422 non-binaries in the USA**.

Compared to cities

Its interesting to compare these numbers to US city population data found at wikipedia.
http://en.wikipedia.org/wiki/List_of_United_States_cities_by_population.

Look over this list and compare it to a city near you or that you know. Spending most of my life in Washington state, cities in this range are Bellevue, Vancouver, Tacoma, and Spokane. These are all major state cities. Though not large enough to fill the top 78 population cities. The transsexual population would be around 6 times larger.

For those of you from another country you can use the interactive map to find similar city sizes in your country at a city population finder. http://www.citypopulation.de/cities.html.

Canada, UK, Australia
These 3 countries are very similar from what I see in TG populations vs the USA. The UMass data would not be able to support the ratio, being a USA based study. Neither will the USA Transsexual population based on Lynn Conway's ratio be applied, since these are based on USA surgeries, so these numbers must have further supporting number and are just guesses applying the same Androgyne ratio. The assumption is that the countries have similar TG communities and normally interact with each other online. Someone else can crunch the numbers and see if the ratio estimates is near or far.

UK - 60,943,912[xvi] (July 2008 est.) 23,704 to 47,427
Canada – 33,424,260[xvii] (Nov 9, 2008 est.) 13,000 to 26,011
Australia – 21,481,389[xviii] (Nov 10, 2008 est.) 8,355 to 16,717

3.1.6 Estimate World Non-Binary Population
Current World populations as of Sept 7, 2008 as I write this is 6,722,043,041. If the ratio holds true for the rest of the world, which factors and accuracy are unknown to me, the population would be between **2,600,000** and **5,200,000**.

3.2 Percentage of Transgender Method
How many transgender persons are non-binary? [xix]
Before I did this book, from a post I gathered data that lead me to an estimated 1 in 10 (10%) of transgender persons are non-binary. My data varied from high 40%, to medium 20%, but I felt the 10% seemed more reasonable, considering the large amount of crossdressers and transsexuals. Though the sources of these numbers have one major problem. In that the crossdressers are for the most part understated in the sources that I gathered the information. So in the end, rather than trying to use 10% of transgender, I will try to find what more realistic percentage of transgender are non-binary.

56

3.2.1 UMass Study[xx]

The survey of 3,474 transgender persons in a online survey did not have non-binary terms for which reasons I believe the surveyors only cared about the transsexuals. Although, it only had male, female, transgender, it also had an "Other" category. This "Other" category had 20% selected which the details I have read indicate those respondents who marked "other" most often identified as "genderqueer," "crossdresser," "androgynous," or "unsure." The surveyors had to type in their identification themselves in the survey, rather than having a choice to select, which they all piled up into a category called "Other". When one removes the unsure, crossdressers and undecided, one could know the number, but the results indicate no such numbers.

Although they do not provide data for how many androgynes and other non binaries answered their survey beyond that 20%, they do have some data that can support an androgyne percentage of population, in the Gender Expression question, from the phone interviews, and e-mails received. The Gender Expression question however is more clear in that 9% selected "other," and most often expressed as "ambiguous," "androgynous," "bigender," "both female and male," "butch," "crossdresser," "fluid," "genderqueer," and "varies."Perhaps the most exact of the numbers, doesn't contain crossdressers or any others, 10% of 118 phone interviews identified as non-binary genders of genderqueer, androgyne, bigender, and both male and female identified, 8% of 301 emails received identified as these same.

From the UMass study around 10% or a little less seems probable for a percentage of non-binaries. And those that did indicate so, had to indicate actively since no option was available as an answer. This number however has problems which I will explain later.

3.2.2 IFGE Poll

My Gender Identity (anonymous)[xxi]

Man	4.13 % (27)
TransMan	9.79 % (64)
Two Spirit	6.88 % (45)
TransWoman	38.84 % (254)
Woman	17.28 % (113)
GenderQueer	4.59 % (30)

57

AGender   ⫿ 1.53 % (10)
I think I need a bigger box! ⬚   ⬚ 16.97 % (111)

     This would seem like a good source of information, however this does not included crossdressers. I will explain the problem later

What is your gender? Poll

Male	**451**	44%
Female	**567**	55%
Other	**9**	1%

Selected other responses: Both, unic, genderqueer

Poll retrieved May 14, 2011 from
http://dailyuw.com/specials/sex2009/poll/

Another way to look at number of non-binaries is comparing it to the other transgender groups.

Estimated Transgender Population

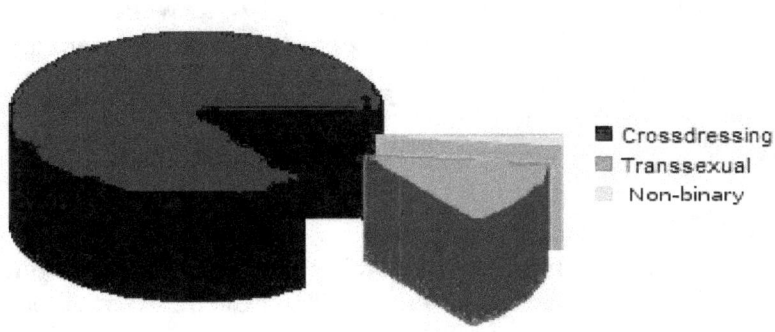

- Crossdressing
- Transsexual
- Non-binary

3.3.1 Crossdressing Population

Current estimate of active serious Crossdressing is %5, which includes all orientations including gay as in drag. Being that crossdressing is almost exclusively male, the male population in July of 2007 148,658,898 male US citizens. **7,432,945** (80.8% to 89.4% of TG) to estimated frequent *USA male crossdressers.* I do not have data on female crossdressers at this time.

3.3.2 Transsexual Population

Using Lynn Conway's ratio adjusted to add the FTMs, there would be **762,721** to **1,525,442** (9.2% to 16.6% of TG) estimated USA transsexuals.

3.3.3 Problem with the original sources for percentage of transgender method

If non-binaries are 10% of TG the formula to find the population of Transgender in the USA using this method would be .90X=8195666 and . 90X= 8958387 equaling 9,106,296 to 9,953,763 equaling 910,630 to 995,376. This number seems much higher than the other method. Which comes to a possible explanation. Normally Crossdressers are not as inclined to be Activists and hang out where as Tses are prevalent. The survey and IFGE are very much activist and very much TS heavy, although they try to include crossdressers somewhat. The IFGE both sources do not even include Crossdressers as major options. IFGE draws more of the lifestyle crossdressers more similar to TS, rather than the closeted more fetish crossdressers or drag. Heterosexual Crossdresser are almost always excluded from homosexual, though the number of crossdressing for population includes both. Rather many crossdressers have their own sources specific to their interests.

Let me show you a crossdresser predominant poll to illustrate my point. At crossdresserheaven.com there is a poll [xxii] that has first of all separates crossdressers (157) from tranvestites (19), as well as the full-time transgenderists (25). Now compare the size of these 3 to the transsexuals (12) and the "Don't try to categorize me" (12), aka "other genders", the genderqueers, androgynes, non-binary, bigender, etc... This shows you how the CD/TV polling in the prior polls is probably under represented .

3.3.4 Reusing Transsexual Ratio Method

Using the ratio non-binary **118,665** to **237, 422** USA non-binary in the USA, which is more realistic than the 10% or even 20% methods which I think creates an overstatement compared to the other transgender groups, for reasons I explained above.

3.3.5 Estimate Total USA Transgender Population

The USA TG population would be **8,314,331** to **9,195,809**, about the population size of New York City or larger than most states except the top 10.

3.3.6 Estimate 1.42% to 2.58% of TG Population as being non-binary

0.0142 (**1.42%**) to 0.0258 (**2.58%**) of TG population seems more accurate when factoring in a more realistic population for crossdressers. Although 10% may be accurate in TS heavy sources, when factoring in crossdressers, I don't think it is reliable.

If I find more accurate different data, of course these numbers will change. It rather is an estimate based off of my current data.

3.5 Using Estimated Non-Binary Gender Population to figure out statistical sample size and confidence for polls and surveys.

In order to try figuring out how accurate the surveys are, and what size survey would be ideal, this section will try to determine this, and explain the assumptions.

In statistics first the population must be known. In this case, I have an estimate range for the total non-binary gender population. I will use this number, but have in mind that if this number is too large for the actual real life population of non-binary gender, the polls and surveys become more accurate. And if this range of numbers is too small, then the data becomes less accurate.

**Estimated Non-Binary Gender/Androgyne/Genderqueer
Population =118,665 to 237, 422**

Possible Error Percentages per sample
For a 95% Confidence Interval

+/-31% a sample size of 10
+/-25% a sample size of 15
+/-20% a sample size of 24
+/-15% a sample size of 43
+/-12% a sample size of 61 to 67
+/-10% a sample size of 84 to 96
+/-9% a sample size of 118 to 119
+/-8% a sample size of 150
+/-7% a sample size of 196
+/-6% a sample size of 266
+/-5% a sample size of 383 to 384
+/-4% a sample size of 597 to 599
+/-3% a sample size of 1058 to 1062

For a 90% Confidence Interval

+/-30% a sample size of 8
+/-25% a sample size of 11
+/-20% a sample size of 17
+/-15% a sample size of 30
+/-10% a sample size of 68
+/-5% a sample size of 272

Ideal target sample size for a +/-5%error

660 (maybe add 6 more just for fun) non-binary gender would be an ideal number of to poll or survey. That is if such a number of non-binary were possible. At that amount the confidence, given the population estimate of non-binary near correct, a 99% confidence interval at +/-5%.

If 660 is not possible, the second and third ideal numbers would be **383** for a 95% confidence interval, or **272** for a 90% confidence interval both at +/-5% error.

Summary
Having now found at least a theoretical population amount for non-binaries, we will now try to look at some common patterns or types of non-binaries according to various behavior, styles, emphasis, and how the view gender. Then certain possible aspects for these types will also be commented on.

What type of non-binary genders are there?

This is one question that I pondered when I decided to poll and find out. Although this list is not complete, it gives a little light how some feel. On can see the variety of ways that those that identify as non-binary feel, think, organize, and relate to the gender binary, continuum, spheres, or spectrum.

4.1 Breaking down the definition(s) of non-binary

In the definitions of non-binary gender identities normally it says "both" male and female or "neither"male nor female. Which from these one can come up with the first four types. Mixed (both), Neither (null), Bigender (both but not mixed and separate persona, and Fluid (changes over time between both or more). Sometimes you will see "beyond", or "outside" gender, which refers to the last major type, the Third Gender.

4.2 Three Polls - Data Concerning % of Non-Binary Major Subdivisions.

What type of androgyne are you?[xxiii]	
Ambigender (both merged), Interdresser, Mixed Gender	24 (38.1%)
Bigender (both separate), Multigender, Plural Gender	10 (15.9%)
Agender (neither) , Neutrois, Nullgender	8 (12.7%)
I am my own Gender (auto-gender).	5 (7.9%)
No choice at this time, Undecided	5 (7.9%)
Fluid (can change, cyclical-gender)	4 (6.3%)
I don't want to be boxed in by labels.	3 (4.8%)
Third Gender (outside all gender, exo-gender, extra-gender,)	2 (3.2%)
None of the above (I will make a post explaining why)	2 (3.2%)

In this chart, Genderqueer option is not available. This site considers Genderqueer more political, activist related rather than gender identity. The some still identify as Genderqueer.

Out of 63 votes the chart breaks it down to subgroups or subcategories of non-binaries. Each of the subgroups emphasizing different feelings or sense of identity.

The largest of the groups being the Mixed/Ambi/Inter Gender meaning emphasizing or recognizing both female and male parts, or wholeness of oneself. Sometimes a few refer to bigender, though not plural, though bigender for the most part means plurality.

The Bigender/Multigender having two (or sometimes more) unique genders with separate persona or identities, sometimes called pluralities or systems.

The Agender/Neutrois/Nullgender representing lack of gender, or a neither male nor female identity.

The Fluid can change or cycle gender identity over a period of time.

Third/exo/extra/transcendental gender feel outside of gender.

Self defined gender, or what I called Auto-Gendered, define themselves.

Then there is those that don't want labels.

And undecided (not that there ever needs to be a decision).

Non-binary Identities[xxiv]

- How to you identify?

Agender (4 votes [6.78%])
Androgyne (22 votes [37.29%])
Bi-gender (5 votes [8.47%])
Genderqueer (10 votes [16.95%])
Neutrois (5 votes [8.47%])
Questioning (10 votes [16.95%])
Other (3 votes [5.08%])

This poll shows Androgyne and Genderqueer as two options on this chart. Androgyne and Genderqueer probably is referred to similar to the ambigender/interdresser/mixed gender of the prior poll. Where as Androgyne and Genderqueer were used in the same way as Non-binary Identities in this poll Also Neutrois and Agender are separate here which are combined in the prior poll. Bigender is in both, though this poll has no mention of Multigender, or Plural gender which is probably more implied.

64

Spiritual Androgyne identities
The next poll was taken from a spiritual androgynous website, though a little info can be taken from it. It also shows some possible meanings of the word Androgyne, as mentioned in the history section. The poll votes are rather low.

Question[xxv]

There are many names and labels out there for folks who are androgynous: some are traditional, some are modern, some are even post-modern. Our self-chosen labels are very important as they represent our sense of identity. Let's explore who we are as the community of androgynes. You may choose as many labels as you'd like. How do you identify?

Responses

Choices	Votes
two spirit	4
nadle, winkte, hijra, galla, or another traditional/cultural word	0
androgyne	7
bi-gendered	2
asexual	0
male OR female	2
neither male nor female	4
fairie	0
queer	2
gay	1
fag	0
intersex	0
transexual	0
dyke	0
other	2

No sample size is given, so 7 is the minimum number of people that took this poll, those that voted for the label "androgyne", which is also the name of the online group.

"Two spirit" an Native American term predominantly, and "neither male nor female" are the next two popular voted labels from these spiritual androgynes. Bi-gendered, "male or female", queer, and other are next followed by gay, then many unchosen labels. These unchosen options show that this poll has too little sampling, considering this is a group of spiritual androgynes bridging many genders and orientations.

4.3 Even smaller subdivisions

Even within these Gender subcategories are variations in types of persons that can emphasis certain aspects of Gender, certainly able to emphasis more than one aspect or even all of them, together with one's gender identity. The main aspects covered in this chapter are Psychological or Cerebral, Social Cultural Behavioral, Communicative, Biological, and Dressing and Appearance. For data and some explanation concerning how I derived these aspects see the next chapter, chapter 5.

4.3.1 Mixed Gender (Ambigendered, Androgyne, Interdresser, Some Genderqueers) (estimated at 40% of non-binaries; see two polls above)

These are those that are "Both" male and female. Masculine and Feminine present and desired in near equal or lage amounts. A notion of 40% to 60% presence of the masculine and feminine mix is sometimes identified.

1. Psychological or Cerebral Mixed Non-Binary- those that are all mentally mixed gender focused. And think, write, or journalize to fit one's gender identity. Many times, one emphasis thinking, philosophies, abstractions, or even something intimate such as poetry, music, or other arts.
2. Social,Cultural, Behavioral Mixed Non-Binary- those that act or behave in mixed gendered ways maybe even influencing one's gender roles in accordance to one's gender identity. This may affect the dynamic interaction of one's relationships, with love interests as well as family, friendships, and colleagues. And also sway the groups and organizations one participates or frequents.
3. Communicative Mixed Non-Binary- those that communicate in mixed gendered ways in accordance to one's gender identity. It may include voice tone and resonance, or just topics and relating to others in mixed gender communication styles and techniques.
4. Biologically Mixed Non-Binary- those that have GID and try to change ones biology mixed gendered or a different ratio of bodily anatomy. This may include doing HRT, breast augmentations/reduction/removal, body hair removal or hormonally induced growth, genital removal/modification/SRS, increase or decrease in muscular build, and/or other bodily modifications. The desire is to have both aspects of physical sex present, much like a natural hermaphrodite.
5. Mixed Gender Dressing and Appearance- those that androgynously dress to fit one's mixed Androgyne Gender Identity. Using both male and female pieces or cosmetics. It can mean binding, jewelry, makeup. They may genderblur, genderfuck, for shock, or more likely desire to dress androgynously, interdress, glam up, or dress "butch"

for oneself, to feel more in tune or sync with hir gender identity.

4.3.2 Neither Gender (Agender, Neutrois, Nullgender, Absence of ⁶⁷ Gender, some Genderqueer).

4.3.2 Neither Gender (Agender, Neutrois, Nullgender, Absence of Gender, some Genderqueer). (An Estimate at 10%-15% of non-binaries; see two polls above). These are those that are "Neither" male and female. They reject both masculine and feminine.

1. Psychological or Cerebral Neither Gender Non-Binary- those that are mentally ungendered or pregendered
2. Social or Cultural Neither Gender Non-Binary- those that act or behave in with no gender focus.
3. Communicative Neither Gender Non-Binary- those that communicate in however they naturally communicate with no gender focus.
4. Biologically Neither Gender Non-Binary (**Neutrois**)- Those that have GID and try to change ones biology to null or without gender. This is where the word Neutrois fits in. A **Neutrois** is someone who identifies as being non-gendered and seeks to lose the major physical signifiers that indicate gender to others (breasts, facial and body hair, crotch bulges, etc).
5. Neither Gender Dressing and Appearance- trying to dress without gender focus. Unisex or universal clothing. May cut hair to a non-gendered appearance.

4.3.3 Bigender (Multigender, Plural Gender, N-Spirited, Systems) (An Estimate at around 10% of non-binaries; see two polls above). These are those that have separate male and female entities, persona, selves, genders in one body. Many times, each of the persons will have a separate names, characteristics, behaviors, and likes/dislikes. The multigendered will be able to shift in and out of the personage with self control most the time. Multigendered are normally conscious of the identities within themselves.

1. Psychological or Cerebral Bigender Non-Binary- Those that are mentally multigendered. They may write using two or more gender selves, sometimes separating the individual dialogs. Its an awareness of the individualistic natures within themselves.
2. Social, Cultural, and Behavioral Bigender Non-Binary- Those that branch out to society and reveal their multigendered selves to society. Behavior can change depending one which person is in charge of the body.
3. Communicative Bigender Non-Binary- Those that communicate with others in one form or another using their multigendered selves. Because of the very nature of the multi genders, those communication styles can vary more from person to person.
4. Biological Bigender Non-Binary- I don't think I have ever heard of

any at the moment, unless it refers to one creating major changes which I have heard hints of.

5. Bigendered Dressing and Appearance- I have heard of individuals dressing masculine, feminine, or androgynous to fit one or more of the persona.

4.3.4 Fluid Gender (some Genderqueers)(An Estimate at around 5% of non-binaries; see the first poll above). This is a person whose gender fluctuates and changes over time. It may be rapidly or over longer periods of time. The person doesn't change persona or identity as in multigender, rather its a person that feels or identifies with gender differently. It may fluctuate to masculine, then feminine, then androgynous, etc.. The changes may be rapid, cyclical, chaotic, or steady. They may have gender flexibility[xxvi] which is more based on mood or environment.

1. Psychological or Cerebral Fluid Non-Binary- Their mental moods, emotions, thoughts, and inner mind gender is in a constant flux.
2. Social, Cultural, and Behavioral Fluid Androgynes- Their Gender behavior changes and is in a flux.
3. Communicative Fluid Non-Binary- One whose communication style, voice, and techniques change gender over time.
4. Biological Fluid Non-Binary- One who pursues bilogical changes over time, reversal, and flux. I have heard of a few of these. May involve hrt, genital surgeries, cosmetic modifications, or cosmetic surgeries. Extremely rare.
5. Fluid Dressing and Appearance- Dress, manner, and appearance fluctuate and change over time

4.3.5 Third Gender (Beyond Gender, Transcendental Gender) (An Estimate at around 3% of non-binaries; see the first poll above) Although this is sometimes culturally and politically defined as a third gender such as Hijras and two-spirits, the essence of being third gender is feeling as though gender has a third gender option, which is separate and distinct from the binary genders male and female. The 5 aspects may vary greatly.

4.3.6 Self-Defined and Unlabeled Genders, Postgender (and a bunch of other labels unique)(An Estimate of around 15% of non-binaries; see the two polls above). The 5 aspects are self-defined.

4.3.7 Undecided (an Estimate of around 10% - 15% of non-binaries; see three polls above)

4.3.8 Other Non-Binary Gender Terms
These are not included in the polls above but you will find them used.

Non-Conforming Gender

Gender Variant

Gender Outlaws

Non-Binary Gender Variant (NBGV)
Non-traditional Gender

Pregender

Postgender

Pangender

Polygender

Omnigender

Genderblur

Genderfuck

4.4 Further Subdivision Male, Female, Intersex Biological Sexes

Finally sex seems to have a role in what emphasis an non-binary gendered person shifts or leans towards. Male born non-binaries are more likely wish to feminize or reduce (eliminate) their masculine traits.

Female born non-binaries are more likely to wish to be masculinized or reduce (eliminate) their feminine traits.

Intersexed born non-binaries are more likely to wish to dwell in the in between state, rather than slide or pick a binary gender.

See chapter 2 data on sexes for further details concerning the population sizes of male, female, and intersexed non-binary gendered persons.

4.5 Summary
Non-binaries can be subdivided into how they relate to the gender-binary or lack of such binary. One's birth sex along with one's Aspects of Gender included in one's current state can be analyzed to better indicate the reasons and motives for such feelings and thinking of individuals or a group of non-binaries.

Chapter 5
Aspects of gender influenced by the non-binary gender identity

The aspects of gender that were in the last chapter came from one inquiry I did to find out more about the non-binary gender identities and the scope that non-binary gender influences.

Also one must remember that birth sex may affect how one is influenced. Male born non-binaries are more likely to be anti-masculine and pro-feminine, and female-born non-binaries are more likely to be anti feminine and pro-masculine. And some may feel pro-mixed gendered, and anti-single gendered. Or some may feel pro-neutral or pro-genderless, and anti-gendered.

5.1 A list of 19 Aspects of persons influenced by non-binary gender

To answer this question a group of non-binaries were asked, "What areas is, might, or will be important to you of a possible adrogynic (non-binary) influence?" The purpose was to see what non-binaries feel gender identity influences in their lives.

Most important in this poll is the order of the votes not the total amount. The total voter shown at the bottom is wrong, since it excludes members having left or been removed from the website, the real total should be about twice the shown amount. So I will exclude that number which should actually be about 30 or more.

[xxvii]What areas is, might, or will be important to you of a possible adrogynic influence? (Vote more than one answer, as many boxes as you want, whatever feels right. Come back and change your votes at any time.)

Area	Votes
Gender Roles: you do or want to allow yourself to doing mixed or undefined gender role activities.	22
Gender Behavior: you do or feel the urge to behave in mixed gender ways.	22
Thinking: do you feel you think in a androgynous way.	19
Character: you do or want to have characteristics that are androgynous.	18
Socially: you do or wish to relate to others as a non polar gender person.	17
Values and Virtues: you do or want to have goals and values that are universal and without gender limit.	16
Gender Identity: you are a non polar gender person.	15
Clothing: you do or want to dress in mixed or neutral clothing.	15
Music, Movies, Entertainment	15
Communication style: you do or wish to have mixed gender	14

communication styles or voice sound.

Intimate Relationship: you do or wish to be involved in a romantic relationship in a non polar way or manner.	13
Hobbies, sports, or interests: your androgyny influences what types you do.	13
Educational: your androgyny helps you and influences the types of knowledge and interests (or barriers you break) in your quest for higher learning.	11
Science: Support or desire scientific information, tests, and research that may help explain or make androgyny understood scientific.	11
Pronouns and Gender References	10
Politically: you androgyny affects who you vote for and what issues are important to you in the political sense.	7
Career: do you feel it influences your occupation.	7
Literary: your androgyny influences what types of authors or stories you read.	5
Religion or Beliefs: you do or want to belong to a group of people with beliefs that support your androgynous beliefs.	5

This is the first data that I have seen anywhere that supports both non-binary being a real and influential gender identity and showing the depth of how this gender influences the non-binary's life. All the other data that I have seen, has just been theoretical, philosophical, or opinionated lacking supporting data.

Comparing the data of this poll I gathered over a year ago to the current data, which is a few more votes higher, we can analyze the results. Then I can use my theoretical, philosophical, or opinionated response armed with real data. And I will comment on the aspects with 10 or greater, not commenting on the bottom four of religion, politics, career, and literary, which I will consider less influenced.

The top two influenced areas are :

Gender Roles: you do or want to allow yourself to doing mixed or undefined gender role activities.

Gender Behavior: you do or feel the urge to behave in mixed gender ways.

These are human actions and reasons for actions. I think they are basically the same thing, except focusing on "who" is the observer. *Gender Behavior* being the non-binary's motivation and urge to behave in a certain way.

Behavior[xxviii]
1. manner of behaving or acting.
2. Psychology, Animal Behavior.
    a. observable activity in a human or animal.
    b. the aggregate of responses to internal and external stimuli.
    c. a stereotyped, species-specific activity, as a courtship dance or startle reflex.
3. Often, behaviors. a behavior pattern.
4. the action or reaction of any material under given circumstances: the behavior of tin under heat.

Whereas the *Gender Roles* would focus on Society or Culture, others, observing the non-binary and making a judgment of what role one is acting out or behaving.

In my opinion, these are two sides of the same coin, behavior and roles, though "who" is the observer and the details of motivation, perspective, judgment, and reasons change. And this is the basis for the subdivision Social or Cultural aspects of the prior chapter.

Next in the list of influenced aspects is:

Thinking: do you feel you think in a androgynous way.

Androgynous in used in this answer doesn't refer to how one looks (a popular definition by many). Rather referring to the adjective androgynous meaning having both or neither masculine and feminine characteristics. This is the basis for psychological or cerebral aspects I mentioned in the last chapter.

This could mean one hasn't developed the division of thinking many binary-gendered persons develops during childhood or adolescence. That is under an assumption that such division into cultural genders occurs, under nurturing, social, or even biological influences.

Character: you do or want to have characteristics that are androgynous.
When I wrote this I was thinking of character attributes like "the aggregate of features and traits that form the individual nature of some person or thing". I have a difficult time explaining or defining character, and I think this topic deserves study and analysis on its own.

Socially: you do or wish to relate to others as a non polar gender person.
In the next section, will emphasize the despair and obstacles non-binaries face when relating to others and being judged by others. This is part of the social and cultural aspects I mentioned in the chapter, together with behavior and roles.

Values and Virtues: you do or want to have goals and values that are universal and without gender limit.
For more information on Values and Virtues see Wikipedia:
>Virtues at http://en.wikipedia.org/wiki/Virtue
>Values at http://en.wikipedia.org/wiki/Values

Gender Identity: you are a non polar gender person.
How one feels about oneself and identifies without binary constriction or with one's own control.

Clothing: you do or want to dress in mixed or neutral clothing.
A self-expression or sometimes a desire to fit a cultural norm or role.

Music, Movies, Entertainment
Receive influences of artistic expressions in accordance to one's non-binary identity.

Gender Biology: you have or desire mixed sexual anatomy.
One may wish to change one's sexual anatomy to be in accordance to one's non-binary identity.

Communication style: you do or wish to have mixed gender communication styles or voice sound.
What style, methods, or techniques using both or neither gender can one use? There have been many books and websites specifically focused on gender communication as well as androgyny in Communication.

Intimate Relationship: you do or wish to be involved in a romantic relationship in a non polar way or manner.
This is a tough one being that most the time, your partner will know, or seem to know, about your non-binary tendencies, either directly or indirectly. Many non-binaries that get into great relationships may feel that their gender identity actually helps out their relationship. Though as you can read in the non-binary fear section, fear of romantic or intimate relationships is tied for

Hobbies, sports, or interests: your androgyny influences what types you do. Stuff like Anime, Manga, online chatting or forums, and online gaming are popular hobbies to express one's non-binary gender identity.

Educational: your androgyny helps you and influences the types of knowledge and interests (or barriers you break) in your quest for higher learning.

Science: Support or desire scientific information, tests, and research that may help explain or make androgyny understood scientific.
For me this is a higher priority especially when dealing with facts and statistical data. I really think that more factual data needs to be published, rather than opinions without evidence.

Pronouns and Gender References
The dislike of he, she, and it. And maybe the preference of sie, zie, hir, ze, mer. Or use of third person non-gendered pronouns of they, them, we, you, one, someone, anyone. Instead of mam or sir (or whatever gendered words your language uses for respect), one can use polite formal language.

5.2 Differences compared to non-binary's birth sex?

Question

What makes you different from (most) people of your birth sex? (tick all that apply to you)[xxix]

Responses

Choices	Votes	%
My interests	22	15
My clothes	21	15
My social behaviour	20	14
My temperament (more typical of the 'other' sex)	19	13
My hair	17	12
Other accessories (jewelry, ties)	16	11
My makeup	12	8
My sexual orientation	11	7

This poll was asked to try figuring out what aspects of gender of non-binary make one different from one's birth sex. This sorta goes along with the aspects influenced by gender.

Interests
The kind of interests we are talking about here is definition #2 in Dictionary.com, "2. something that concerns, involves, draws the attention of, or arouses the curiosity of a person ." In order to be of interest, there must be of spark of desire, need, enjoyment, along to give birth to the interest. A motivation based on basic needs.

Interests cover a broad range of fields in psychology. Some of these fields are the studies of emotions, cognition, development, education, aesthetics, personality, and motivations.

One can study some of the basic theories and concepts of interests and motivation by keyword searching Motivation Psychology, or by visiting some of the links presented in this chapter's endnotes.[xxx]

Basically these are saying that they have different interests than their birth sex. Meaning their attention is drawn away from things normally attributed to their birth sex to things outside or beyond normal birth gender interests.

Clothing
One may be surprised that clothing is rated so high in non-binary differences compared to birth gender. Normally the philosophy or rational followed is that one wants to show or experience a external version of their inner gender. This in one sense could mean adornment such as clothing. Three other gender expressions of physical appearance items are listed on this list, however it is ranked as the highest of the four: followed by hair and accessories, then lastly makeup.

Social-Behavior
How one presents themselves in social context can break the normal gender norms.
Temperament
Temperament refers to how one thinks, behaves, and reacts.

Hair
Normally the non-binary that I hear talking about hair concerns either female-born or male born focused. Female-born normally are concerned with getting more masculine, androgynous, or neutral hair cuts. Or trying to add facial hair through HRT or other means. Male-born normally are concerned with achieving a more feminine, androgynous,

or neutral hair cuts. Or preventing hair loss. Also one may wish to remove or add body or facial hair, temporary or permanent. Such decisions are left to the individual, rather than broad sweeping community wide such as with Tses.

More details can be found in chapters 2 and 4 concerning the last few poll data, concerning cosmetics, fashion, and orientation.

The next 4 chapters will concern non-binary obstacles, fears, inequalities, and anti-non-binary arguments; a section on confusion, fear, hate, and discrimination.

Part 2 Issues of Other Genders

Chapters 6 through 14

What obstacles do you face as a non-binary?

1.) Figuring out who and what you are. There are very few easily available resources for androgynes and it's hard to even find the word unless you know it first. I came across it by chance. — 13

2.) Androgyny isn't a well-known term, and therefore when/if you do want to explain your gender-identity you will need at least an hour after which the most popular reply you will gain is "I don't get it..." — 12

3) Lack of ability to associate with other genders, and not even fully with other Androgynes (due to the individualistic natures) which can lead to a sense of 'loneliness'. — 11

4.) The path is not laid down in a set path. The way varies from person to person. The results will be different for each individual. The manner may be very different. The definitions may be unique and individual, as well as less defined. — 11

5.) One can fluctuate in their gender identity. Which may range from acceptable and expected to confusion and alarm. — 11

6.) You generally have to pick a "binary" pronoun and identity for use in the workplace. — 10

7. Seeing things that the binaries do not, such as 'gender games' between the binaries. i don't know about you others, but I always want to kick these people in the groin. It is so irritating. — 10

8.) Knowing that you can either "pick one" or be totally open with everyone--there is never any going stealth or just being yourself without any questions. — 9

9.) In what information that one does find, one must stay grounded in the true self inner voice. Its true of everything, but a few have written posts about getting lost or feeling lost. — 8

10.) The fact that transition may start, but it never really ends. There is no finish line. You never make it through transition, it is an on-going thing. — 8

11.) Orientation can become a difficult concept to consider. Rather the whole idea of orientation might be thrown out the window, or simplified to an individual basis. — 8

12.) Because SRS is generally not something most androgynes seek, (would different plumbing really change how I feel about myself?), it can be hard to explain why one may want to look like the opposite sex yet not be. "Oh yeah, zie looks like a girl — 8

13.) understanding what being androgyne actually means is the hardest part, a transsexual can say they are the other sex and even if the extent of this identification or the trouble with deciding on what they will do about it, they know what it means to be one. — 7

14.) One I have heard more than once is something like "Am I a transsexual that hasn't decided to transition, nor felt the full urge. And am I just holding on the the last threads of my unwanted gender. Or do I embrace both or reject both." — 7

15.) If you require surgical or hormonal alteration, you generally have to pay high for black market type stuff or lie like an sob and pretend to be ftm or mtf. — 6

16.) Based on my personal experience; my family-member simply 'brushed it off' when I told her I was Androgyne, and didn't believe it was significant or affecting my life. — 5

17.) There is no null-hormone.   📖 5

18.) Being told by "real" transsexuals and "real" transgendered people that androgyne is a "cop-out" gender identity for people who want the best of both worlds. That it's the "easy way out." Bull.   📖 5

19.) Trying to understand those that limit their gender behavior to just one polar. After experiencing unlimited gender behavior and expressions, only focusing on one is unthinkable to me. Its more like "why?"   📖 5

20.) Even if you allow yourself to have mixed gender identity (s) in the public or among friends/family, if you focus on one for certain situations, then you get a reverse judgment. Instead of amazing them with mixed gender, they wonder why you are focusing on that particular gender.   📖 4

21.) Your guy friends don't believe you when tell them that even though you look and act feminine, that you are not gay.   📖 4

22.) When your guy friends decide you're hot, then when you tell them "Look, I'm not a girl, I'm gonna change aspects of myself" they start saying "YOU TURNED ME GAY!!"   📖 3

23.) The strange argument I've encountered on some message boards where male-bodied androgynes claim that females cannot be androgyne.   📖 1

6.1 A list of 23 non-binary Obstacles Rated and Comments

1.) Figuring out who and what you are. There are very few easily available resources for androgynes and it's hard to even find the word unless you know it first. I came across it by chance.

This is my attempt at helping along these lines. For a while, doing PR for non-binaries was something a few were recommending. Just to get our name out there. From YouTube video, to wikipedia update, to table discussions, to news articles. These works here in this book are one of my responses to try making available a resource for non-binaries.

2.) Androgyny isn't a well-known term, and therefore when/if you do want to explain your gender-identity you will need at least an hour after which the most popular reply you will gain is "I don't get it..."

I think helping out with the first concern may or may not help with this second concern. Getting the term out there, if the community continues to agree or use the term. Population rarity of non-binaries has hindered such individuals from gathering in any particular area, although they were always there. Only recently with the Internet, the pathway to gather smaller groups world wide is available.

With some PR, might not help them "get" how you feel, though it will help them possibly hear the term more. I hope more will have the courage to come out in public ways. I am thankful for those that have already braved the public light, in any small way on up to greater ways.

3) Lack of ability to associate with other genders, and not even fully with other Androgynes (due to the individualistic natures) which can lead to a sense of 'loneliness'.

Although I believe the population of non-binaries will increase, I am not sure if doing so will decrease loneliness. It may for some of us, but the individualistic natures may keep even increase in population separate somewhat.

4.) The path is not laid down in a set path. The way varies from person to person. The results will be different for each individual. The manner may be very different. The definitions may be unique and individual, as well as less defined.

Maybe some organization(s) could standardize some terms, and identify some common pathways. Such undertaking would require analysis of a large group of non-binaries. But as I have learned even in this writing, there are always exceptions and individual feelings or opinions.

The APA hasn't mentioned anything about non-binaries, that I know of at this time.

I am not familiar with anything major from any of the other governing or influential organizations such as IFGE, GenderPac, or Gender.org. They seem to be focused on being GLBTI organizations which seems to be where all the money is located, seeing the large donations from mainly Gay and Lesbian Doners.

WPATH is focused on TS , mostly binary transitioning information, with only small references to "other" genders.

Crossdressing Organizations like http://www.tri-ess.org/ are focused on their own issues.

5.) One can fluctuate in their gender identity. Which may range from acceptable and expected to confusion and alarm.

Many non-binaries that I know experience or have experienced moments when they feel their gender identity is changing. Honestly, sometimes their gender identity does change dramatically. Many times I have seen it return after a period of time, from days, weeks, to months.

6.) You generally have to pick a "binary" pronoun and identity for use in the workplace.

Although one may prefer gender neutral pronouns and identity at home, online, or among other non-binaries, one must work in order to survive and earn an income. And using gender neutral pronouns may beyond one's ability, fears, reality, or expectation.

7.) Seeing things that the binaries do not, such as 'gender games' between the binaries. i don't know about you others, but I always want to kick these people in the groin. It is so irritating.
This seems funny but is true. The non-binary perspective can be quite different then a Cisgendered.

8.) Knowing that you can either "pick one" or be totally open with everyone-- there is never any going stealth or just being yourself without any questions.
This depends on if one is psychologically/cerebral focused only, or has influence of non-binary external expressions. For those with outward expressions, at the current time period in most cultures, there will be questions. And one will not "Pass" or have any "Stealth" ability. Which leads to two extremes of picking one or being open, with options in between.

9.) In what information that one does find, one must stay grounded in the true self inner voice. Its true of everything, but a few have written posts about getting lost or feeling lost.
One can be thrown off by the new information presented by anyone, my works and research included. Having said that, I hope others reading this will realize that my own hopes for you is to stay grounded in your true self, and don't let anything in here or any of my other works (or any others works) throw your own sense of self off, or conflict with your inner voice.

Unless your against non-binaries, lol. Which case I hope you have a change of heart and are warmed to the feelings, ideas, and experiences of such gender diverse persons.

10.) The fact that transition may start, but it never really ends. There is no finish line. You never make it through transition, it is an on-going thing.
This is especially true for Gender Fluid Non-Binaries. And may be true of everyone. People change over the years and they transition different phases of their lives. Sometimes dramatically, other times slightly.

11.) Orientation can become a difficult concept to consider. Rather the whole idea of orientation might be thrown out the window, or simplified to an individual basis.

When one considers themselves both or neither gender, and one is attracted to someone else with a gender, whatever it may mean, current orientation lacks words to describe this relationship.

12.) Because SRS is generally not something most androgynes seek, (would different plumbing really change how I feel about myself?), it can be hard to explain why one may want to look like the opposite sex yet not be. "Oh yeah, zie looks like a girl

This deals with an non-binary approach to sex and gender. Separating how one looks from how they feel about themselves. And the cultural or role limits and norms placed on people.

13.) understanding what being androgyne actually means is the hardest part, a transsexual can say they are the other sex and even if the extent of this identification or the trouble with deciding on what they will do about it, they know what it means to be one.

The confusion of terms is one aspect that makes being an non-binary confusing.

14.) One I have heard more than once is something like "Am I a transsexual that hasn't decided to transition, nor felt the full urge. And am I just holding on the the last threads of my unwanted gender. Or do I embrace both or reject both."

This is something I have seen a few times. Sometimes it is true. Other times I think its not so true, citing several Transsexuals that have realized they are non-binary after HRT and SRS.

15.) If you require surgical or hormonal alteration, you generally have to pay high for black market type stuff or lie like an sob and pretend to be ftm or mtf.

This is an unfortunate fact unless one is lucky.

16.) Based on my personal experience; my family-member simply 'brushed it off' when I told her I was Androgyne, and didn't believe it was significant or affecting my life.

I can see how they might have apathy or insignificance. I think some might think it is a phase, which to some might be a phase. The ages around college level show higher population then the steady population of other ages according to the poll I mentioned earlier. I don't know if its accounted by being a phase, or the time and ability to spend online and devote that time to gender awareness and communication.

17.) There is no null-hormone.
I think what the author of this questioned means is there is no hormone to remove gender traits. Only hormones to increase masculine or feminine features.

18.) Being told by "real" transsexuals and "real" transgendered people that androgyne is a "cop-out" gender identity for people who want the best of both worlds. That it's the "easy way out." Bull.
There sometimes is bad blood between non-binaries and some transsexuals, if in the past the two cross with conflict. Being an non-binary is not easy at all, unless maybe its entirely cerebral and psychological, hidden from others.

Publicly showing non-binary behavior or expressions is not easy unless one is totally secure with oneself, with great self esteem. Either that or just fearless, without care or concern.

19.) Trying to understand those that limit their gender behavior to just one polar. After experiencing unlimited gender behavior and expressions, only focusing on one is unthinkable to me. Its more like "why?"
When one is open to all options, limiting options is unthinkable or hard to go back to. Even if one once did limit their gender behavior and expressions.

20.) Even if you allow yourself to have mixed gender identity (s) in the public or among friends/family, if you focus on one for certain situations, then you get a reverse judgment. Instead of amazing them with mixed gender, they wonder why you are focusing on that particular gender.
I know this is true if I focus on a single behavior or expression. Like going to work, or dressing up for a special reason or event, or just getting my picture taken.

21.) Your guy friends don't believe you when tell them that even though you look and act feminine, that you are not gay.
I hear this one sometimes. I have seen it for female born non-binaries as well when talking about looking or acting masculine. I sorta common for both when and is a fear that many times prevents one from trying any behavior, even if they might want to express something.

84

What are your fears that cause trouble, hesitation, discomfort, blockage, nightmares, inaction, inability to accept, social fears, and / or physical fears?	
Fear of Rejection [disapproval, being ignored] from Others. [family, friends, work, partner, society, religion, other groups, world]	11 (13.3%)
Fear of being Labeled [defined by others, being held hostage by definitions, inability to be unique]	7 (8.4%)
Romantic and intimate relationship fears	7 (8.4%)
Fear of Expression [inability to communicate to others about self, shyness, feeling of being judged, held hostage in solitude or in own home]	6 (7.2%)
Fear of Violence [Fear of being physically harmed, molested, raped, or killed]	6 (7.2%)
Fear from feeling Guilty	6 (7.2%)
Fear of the Unknown	5 (6%)
Financial fears	5 (6%)
Fear of Authoritative Figure [Parent, Boss] [being told or forced what to do , being embarrassed]	5 (6%)
Fear of Pain [feeling pain, hurt, depressed, alone, lost, confused.]	5 (6%)
Fear of Taking Risk with negative result [Failure, making mistake, being judge, repeating past mistake]	4 (4.8%)
Fear of my body (Body parts, Image, anatomy)	3 (3.6%)
Fear of Self-Rejection or Self-Acceptance [Suicidal thoughts]	3 (3.6%)
Fear of Being TS or CD [not Androgyne]	3 (3.6%)
Fear of Self Success. [self-sabotage, procrastination, negative thinking]	3 (3.6%)
I have no fears	2 (2.4%)
Fearing my lack of fear	1 (1.2%)
Fear of Event	1 (1.2%)
Fear of Object [Something related to Androyne]	0 (0%)

7.1 A list of 19 non-binary fears rated and comments

Fearless non-binaries

Of the 13 non-binaries responding to this poll, two were fearless.

Except one of the two has a fear of lacking fears, ironically.

Fear of Rejection [disapproval, being ignored] from Others. [family, friends, work, partner, society, religion, other groups, world]

Number one fear of non-binaries by far, and may be similar, though

probably more intense than other minorities in cultures. Every non-binary, except 2 that have no fears, had this fear in the poll.

With lack of tolerance, narrow mindedness, and anti-doctrines or opinions, one cannot blame such great fear. Especially given that one must succeed or at least participate in a such potentially hostile social Environment .Friends and Family may abandon, become hostile, or oppose one.

expressing non-binary like thoughts, behaviors, or actions. A partner may leave a non-binary revealing hir feelings of gender identity. Work may discriminate an open non-binaries, treating them with unequal treatment. Religions may have anti-trans or non-binary opinions or policies causing conflict among even a service one has participated in for several years.

Fear of being Labeled [defined by others, being held hostage by definitions, inability to be unique]
Just over half of non-binaries with fears have this fear. Labels have a way boxing in one's self. They sorta cage and limit one's actions sometimes, unless one is totally free of judgment.

Romantic and intimate relationship fears
Just over half of non-binaries with fears have this fear. This fear I have seen in different versions. The most common fear is the non-binary's gender identity causing to break apart a relationship.

Another version is that being non-binary for someone single seemingly will mean that sie will be alone forever.

Fear of Expression [inability to communicate to others about self, shyness, feeling of being judged, held hostage in solitude or in own home]
About half of non-binaries with fears have fear of expression. Inability to communicate to others about their non-binary selves. With fear of being judged poorly about such expressed selves.

Fear of Violence [Fear of being physically harmed, molested, raped, or killed]
About half of non-binaries with fears have fear of violence. With concerns of being physically harmed, molested, raped, or even killed.

Fear from feeling Guilty
About half of non-binaries with fears experience a guilt which in turn created fear.

Financial fears
Just under half of non-binaries with fears experience financial fears

Fear of Authoritative Figure [Parent, Boss] [being told or forced what to do , being embarrassed]

Just under half of non-binaries with fears express fears of a authoritative figure. These Authoritative figures have power over living conditions, income, and sometimes security.

Fear of Pain [feeling pain, hurt, depressed, alone, lost, confused.]
Just under half of non-binaries with fears have fear of pain. This fear isn't specific, rather it is connected to other reasons that create pain. But the possibility of feeling pain or getting hurt itself can cause discomfort and disable one, even to fearing anything that might bring such result.

Fear of the Unknown
Unknown futures can be scary. Or the results of traveling a path can be difficult or impossible to predict. Fear of the unknown is another strong fear.

Fear of Taking Risk with negative result [Failure, making mistake, being judge, repeating past mistake]
A third of non-binaries have a fear of taking risks.

Fear of my body (Body parts, Image, anatomy)
A quarter of non-binaries have a fear of their bodies.

Fear of Self-Rejection or Self-Acceptance [Suicidal thoughts]
A quarter of non-binaries have a fear of self-rejection, self-acceptance, on up to possible suicidal thoughts.

Fear of Being TS or CD [not Androgyne]
A quarter of non-binaries have a fear of actually ending up being transsexual or crossdressers, not non-binaries. In that they might not actually belong in the non-binary community, rather in one of the other two. Based on the obstacles poll, its more likely being transsexual as being the fear. I have never heard of someone fearing of being a crossdresser.

Fear of Self Success. [self-sabotage, procrastination, negative thinking]
A quarter of non-binaries actually have a fear of getting what they want, of achieving their desires. And may self-sabotage themselves to prevent themselves from getting it. It may cause them to procrastinate important things. And instead of a positive outlook, negative thinking may rule.

Fear of Event
The lowest fear, only one has, is of some event.

Non-Binaries Unequal Treatment.

Looking at at the http://www.nctequality.org website, I was wondering how androgynes fare when it comes to equality.

Do you ever feel like others are talking about you behind your back. ⬜ 16

Have you experienced verbal abuse because of being androgyne. ⬜ 13

Have you experienced gender stereotyping limiting your abilities as an person. ⬜ 11

Have you experienced unwanted physical touching or body contact because of being androgyne. ⬜ 10

Have you been harassed because of being androgyne. ⬜ 8

Have you ever faced work place discrimination. Unfair, unequal, wrongful termination, uneasiness, being held back from promotions. From your gender identity, expression, communication, behavior, thinking, or beliefs. ⬜ 7

Have you ever experienced physical violence because of being androgyne. ⬜ 5

Have you been asked to leave somewhere only because you are androgyne. ⬜ 4

Have you been raped because of being androgyne. ⬜ 3

Have you experienced inability to marry another partner only because of your being androgyne. ⬜ 2

Have you experienced difficulty traveling because of you being androgyne. ⬜ 2

Have you been denied any public service because of being androgyne. ⬜ 1

Have you had problems with health service, health insurance, care, or medicines only because you are androgyne ⬜ 1

Are you homeless only because you are androgyne. ⬜ 1

Have you experienced difficulty in the military because you are androgyne. ⬜ 1

8.1 A list of 15 Non-Binary Inequalities and Discrimination

Do you ever feel like others are talking about you behind your back. Although people experience gossip and talking behind one's back regardless of gender, those non-binary that have different behavior, characteristics, appearances, or expressions have extra ammo for others to gossip about.

Have you experienced verbal abuse because of being androgyne.
Curse words, vulgar language, belittling especially about one's gender can be cruel. Which purpose is only to cause pain and make lesser ones stance.

Have you experienced gender stereotyping limiting your abilities as an person.
Gender can limit, especially with social peer pressure. Going against the grain can be rough. Unless one is strong enough, stereotypes will limit your abilities as a person. People will try to limit your abilities and tell you what you should or should not be.

Have you experienced unwanted physical touching or body contact because of being androgyne.

No one should experience unwanted physical touch.

Have you been harassed because of being androgyne.
Just because someone has a different gender identity, doesn't give others the right to harass them.

Have you ever faced work place discrimination. Unfair, unequal, wrongful termination, uneasiness, being held back from promotions. From your gender identity, expression, communication, behavior, thinking, or beliefs.

In this day and age, with all the strides made, for non-binaries it continues to be a problem.

Have you ever experienced physical violence because of being androgyne.
Why does this happen. Uncalled for and barbaric.

Have you been asked to leave somewhere only because you are androgyne.
What makes non-binaries so threatening?

Have you been raped because of being androgyne.

Criminality sometimes left not prosecuted.

Have you experienced inability to marry another partner only because of your being androgyne.

State, province, or region law can affect this as well as personal preference.

Have you experienced difficulty traveling because of you being androgyne.
Many difficulties.

Anti Non-Binary Gender

In this chapter we will explore mostly the anti-non-binary gender viewpoints, covering the different aspects non-binaries revealed as important and influenced by their gender identity in chapters 4 and 5.

Anti-Non-Binary Gender

9.1 Culture of Androgeny

The first Article to look at the major points discussed by the author Lee Grady.

> Does anyone remember **a time in America when men were men, women were women, and the children could tell the difference?**
>
> In case you haven't noticed, **the entertainment industry and the educational establishment have teamed up in the last few years to try their best at destroying traditional sex roles.** We are told that in this enlightened era we need to learn to be **"gender neutral." Men are encouraged to explore their "feminine side"; women are pressured to get out into the working world and fight their way up the corporate ladder.**

Next

> If this confusing trend continues, a trend which author George Gilder calls **"the androgynous agenda,"** then America's sexual landscape is going to be **drastically marred beyond recognition** in a few more years.

Next

> George Gilder, who chronicles this erosion of the sex roles in his excellent book Men and Marriage, says the trend should alarm us: "Every year's statistics break the previous records and ever more graphic images arise to signal the **passing of the sexual concepts of masculine and feminine** on which Americans have **based their lives and expectations.**" But why is it that we are experiencing this **sex role crisis**?
>
> **Cultural Bone Rot**

George Gilder calls it **sexual suicide**. It could also be called **God's cultural judgment**.

Next

It is explained very simply in a Bible passage penned by the Apostle Paul, which he wrote to the Christians in Rome at a time when the imperial capital was well on its way to becoming an androgynous society. In this classic epistle he describes in detail the fate of a culture which rejects God's authority and His immutable laws:

"For even though they knew God, they did not honor Him as God, or give thanks; but they became futile in their speculations, and their foolish heart was darkened. Professing to be wise, they became fools ...

Lets fill in what belongs after the ... since the author removed it. ", and exchanged the glory of the immortal God for images made to look like mortal man and birds and animals and reptiles".

Therefore God gave them over in the lusts of their hearts to impurity, that their bodies might be dishonored among them ...

Again lets fill in the ... left out by the author. "They exchanged the truth of God for a lie, and worshiped and served created things rather than the Creator—who is forever praised. Amen."

"For this reason God gave them over to degrading passions; for their women exchanged the natural function for that which is unnatural, and in the same way also the men abandoned the natural function of the woman and burned in their desire towards one another, men with men committing indecent acts and receiving in their own persons the due penalty of their error" (portions of Romans 1:21-27).

And lets finish the chapter with the remaining information which brings further details, which the author did not provide.

28Furthermore, since they did not think it worthwhile to retain the knowledge of God, he gave them over to a depraved mind, to do what ought not to be done. 29They have become filled with every kind of wickedness, evil, greed and depravity. They are full of envy, murder, strife, deceit and malice. They are gossips, 30slanderers, God-haters, insolent, arrogant and boastful; they invent ways of doing evil; they disobey their parents; 31they are senseless, faithless, heartless, ruthless. 32Although they know God's righteous decree that those who do such things deserve death, they not only continue to do these very things but also approve of those who practice them.

This passage outlines **the systematic breakdown of sex roles and the entire family structure itself - a structure which God designed to be the foundation of a healthy society.** In a culture where men have rejected God's government and refused to submit to His moral requirements, **a process of decay** is set in motion. This **moral entropy** begins in the minds of men; as **God's enlightening presence and protective influence is withdrawn**, a pall of **intellectual confusion** settles over the society as a whole.

This **intellectual depravity**, as it progresses in intensity, brings about a **twisting and a perverting of all that is natural and normal.** And if we interpret Paul's comments to the Romans correctly, it would appear that **sexual habits and roles are the ultimate target of this cultural bone rot process.** When a society has divorced itself from God, the final result will be that **men stop being men, women stop being women, and the institutions of marriage and family are destroyed.**

When Paul tells us that men and women "abandon their natural function," this does not simply refer to homosexuality. What is "natural" for woman? Most assuredly her natural instinct is to **marry, bear children, and devote much of her life to nurturing those children.** In an anti-Christian society, women abandon these instincts. They revolt against the concept of childbearing, either through abortion or through neglect of nurturing responsibilities.

What is natural for the man? The most natural, God-given male instinct is for a man to **give himself to one woman as her lifetime sexual partner in marriage, providing for her and for the children which they produce together.** Whenever a civilization revolts against God, men simultaneously revolt against the institution of marriage.

The⁹⁴ article then attacks Sweden for its economic gender neutrality policies.

And the conclusion or call to action

> **We cannot allow maleness and femaleness to drift together into a vague, unisexual zone of neutrality.** We cannot allow monogamous marriage to become just one of several legally accepted lifestyles. We cannot allow federal economic policies to cripple and dismember the family structure.
>
> Returning to pro-family policies will not be easy. It will require **real men** to **stand up** in the public arena to **challenge the anti-gender activists.** It will demand **real women** to **defend** the paramount **role of traditional motherhood.** But we cannot sit idly by while the **social scientists plan America's sexual suicide**. The culture which **refuses to acknowledge** and **honor** the **differences between the sexes will neuter itself**, and ultimately **fade away** into a **childless oblivion**.

9.2 The Case Against Androgynous Marriage

The next article I will look at is one by Steven Rhoads called "The Case Against Androgynous Marriage".

> Two leading family experts, Frank Furstenberg and Andrew Cherlin, find that "over time, the vast majority of children [of divorce] will have little or no contact with their fathers." **So if we care about the future of our kids, we should care about finding the secrets to marriages that last through "sickness and health," through "better and worse."**
>
> These traditional phrases from church weddings might remind **one of the traditional Christian understanding of marriage—one where wives "submit" to the "servant" leadership of their husbands.** Last summer the Southern Baptists reminded the faithful of this Biblical teaching, and feminists denounced it as "domestic feudalism."
>
> Most of the rest of America shrugged it off. After all, **androgyny is everywhere.** Women fly jets and make up 43 percent of all law school graduates. Men go to hair stylists and wear earrings. **To most**

of us, male headship seems like something from another planet.

Next

But social science research on intact marriages finds that in real marriages, **male headship is simply a fact.** Most men and women **seek things in a mate** that render something like male headship **inevitable**.

Next

 Men won't do their share of **housework and child care.** In the typical two-earner family they contribute about **half as much** housework as their employed wives and **less than half as much** solo child care.

Next

When husbands make more than wives, **both say** the husband's job is the more important, but when wives earn more, **neither spouse** says the wife's job is more important. Indeed, such wives are **more likely than other married women to leave the labor force or move to a lower position.** At home these high-achieving wives attempt to be **especially attractive and sexual for their husbands,** and they report indulging husbands' whims and salving egos. When husbands are more dependent on their wives' incomes, **the husbands do very little additional housework.**

Next

Last but not least, a number of the androgynes share some of the Tess-and-Kevin problem. Schwartz notes that **their intimacy and familiarity make them feel more like siblings than lovers.** They were more likely than other couples to "forget to include sex in their daily lives." "Women had fantasies of being taken or mildly dominated," and one complained of a husband who began treating her "too darn respectfully." Many of the peer couples, though, thought they had terrific sex lives, often because they adopted different personas in the bedroom. Schwartz suggested therapy for those who could not "transcend their identities in everyday life" by separating their days from their nights.

Ordinary women show the attractions of male power by making the romance novel the most popular form of fiction in the world. About half of all mass market paperback sales in the country are romance novels. **The hero in the romance novel is always a man with power; the heroine seldom has worldly power.**

Next

In real life, most women do not seem to want **equal worldly power.** Even professional women want the man to be chief provider, not only because they believe the husband's work is more important to his sense of self, but also because they need their husbands **to be successful.**

Next

Finally, most women with full-time jobs **do not resent their double shift.** Despite the imbalance in housework and child care, the majority of wives think the division of labor is fair. Husbands and wives tend to define equality in marriage as **mutual respect, commitment, and reciprocity** over time, rather than as an equal division of tasks.

Next

The androgyny advocates believe that with different social conditioning, men can be reprogrammed to become fully intimate, communicative partners like their wives. And once reprogrammed, men will gain from the sharing of problems as women do. But the testosterone research suggests otherwise. So too does a study that followed the progress of patients dismissed from hospitals after recovery from congestive heart failure. For women the **absence of emotional support in the community** increased their death rates more than eightfold. For men it made no difference at all.

Another study—part of the world-famous Framingham research— suggests **women who bring office problems home may kill off husbands before they're properly feminized.** It seems husbands of white-collar wives with unsupportive bosses are more than three times more likely to die of heart disease, apparently as a result of frustration: Men do not like to talk about unresolvable problems;

women do. The men wanted to protect their wives from hostile bosses but felt unable to help.

Next

The average woman's innate attachment to and skill with babies would, by itself, be more than enough to sink the androgyny project since most men cannot match women in either the attachment or the skill. Mothers everywhere, in all cultures, take care of young children. This seems to be true even in alternative family forms such as communal living groups and unmarried couples.

Next

Women's **keener sense of touch** makes them more responsive to babies, and **their high, sing-song voices** have been shown to be more pleasing than men's attempts at baby talk. Especially pleasing is a mother's voice. Babies hear it in utero, and after birth its sound slows, calms, and steadies a baby's heart.

Next

These figures do not point to an androgynous future, and if we want strong marriages we should be delighted. The richest discussion of American men and women's reasons for divorce, Catherine Riessman's Divorce Talk, finds **women divorcing men who do not work steadily at good jobs**; in parallel fashion **men divorce women when they fall down as homemakers**. Philip Blumstein and Pepper Schwartz's major work, American Couples, finds exactly the same thing. Women are much more likely to divorce men who are not ambitious, whereas men are more likely to divorce women who are ambitious. Men divorce wives if they think the wives are not doing their share of the housework. Women do not divorce men if the men do less housework than they would like them to.

Next

One might wonder why women care so much about marrying in the first place. **Men are obstinately resistant to female influence.** Experiments have found that boys pay no attention when girls tell them to stop doing something and that men pay less attention to a taped message if the voice is a female's. Husbands will push their wives to change things they don't like about their behavior but will resist similar requests on the grounds that "it's just the way I am."

Finally

> Still another large study on sexuality has found that **the women most likely to achieve orgasm each and every time are conservative Protestants.** So if we put it all together, it looks as if the more traditional and religious woman, far from being a serf in "domestic feudalism," is the **most likely to have a mate who shares housework and satisfies her sexually.**

9.3 Against Androgyny (in Marriage)

Androgyny. One of the more popular buzzwords of the 1980's (About Men: "Against Androgyny," Dec. 11). In questioning its value as a panacea for couples in troubled relationships, Michael Norman sounds a reasonable note of caution. Traditional masculine and feminine variations add spice to the stew. In suggesting, however, that androgyny may be responsible for the dissolution of marriages when "disaffected" wives "simply become bored" with their androgynous (read monotonous) husbands, he goes too far.

Those disenchanted wives may be leaving boring relationships not because of the androgynous personalities of their spouses, but because their own androgynous qualities have provided them with alternatives to remaining in undesirable marriages.

Against Learned Androgyny
9.4 Can We Make Boys and Girls Alike?

Summary and Conclusion

> **From either a biological or cultural point of view, then, the feminist project of androgyny is ultimately doomed.** But that doesn't mean that it can't do harm in the meantime. In America, many boys are slipping behind in school; their sisters are significantly more likely to go on to college. Yet thanks largely to the influence of academic feminists, legal and educational resources still flow disproportionately to supposedly victimized girls. In the end, gender won't disappear, whatever the mavens of women's studies hope, but the careers of some bright young men probably will.

Beginning

The intellectual cornerstone of women's studies is **"gender,"** the notion that **differences** between men and women are **not rooted in biology,** as Summers had hypothesized some might be, but are cultural artifacts, inculcated by an oppressive patriarchal society. Precisely because the gender idea builds a specific (radical) political orientation into the field, Patai and Koertge point out, women's studies proved intellectually suspect from the start. You can read that radical politics right in the National Women's Studies Association constitution: "Women's Studies . . . is equipping women to transform the world to one that will be free of all oppression . . . [and is] a force which furthers the realization of feminist aims." True justice for these radical feminists means **overcoming gender** and establishing an **androgynous society.** So when **Summers asserted that something besides artificial cultural roles—something besides "gender"— might account for the distinct positions of men and women in society,** he was undermining the intellectual and political foundation of the entire women's studies establishment.

The alternatives to feminist orthodoxy don't end with Summers-style invocations of biology as destiny. Take psychiatrist Leonard Sax's new book, *Why Gender Matters: What Parents and Teachers Need to Know About the Emerging Science of Sex Differences*, for example. Sax begins by arguing that **variations in how boys and girls learn result from brain biology.** But, unlike many believers in hardwired sex differences, he goes on to argue that **we can triumph over biology through single-sex education.** If we teach boys and girls separately and in sync with their biologically based learning styles, he claims, they will perform equally well in all academics, including math.

There's also a fourth possible view on the relations between sex and success—one that no one has systematically articulated to date. If those who assert biological differences between the sexes disagree about whether we can overcome them, the same might apply to those who assert the power of cultural differences. **Even if we do provisionally hold that virtually all differences between men and women are cultural, might it not also be true that those** differences are impossible to overcome? If so, it wouldn't be₈₉ "gender" but the feminist effort to eliminate it that is truly oppressive. This fourth view suggests that **the very same cultural forces that make feminists desire androgyny may actually prevent us from achieving it. The cultural sources of "gender" difference, properly understood, would then inform us not that our gender identities are infinitely malleable but that they're effectively impossible to change.**

Sociologists have thought long and hard about the cultural "reproduction of society"—the transmission of deeply held cultural attitudes across the generations. Some social thinkers focus on the conscious transmission of cultural messages through **religion and custom**, while others highlight the influence of deeper social structures, such as **economic organization or family forms.** The most sophisticated feminist theories of gender—those that offer the most plausible alternatives to biological explanations—take the latter view. To explain the reproduction of gender differences, they zero in on **family structure**, especially during the first months and years of life, to a time when the way we care for children is far more important than the words we speak.

If we could just break the association between gender and child care, thinks Chodorow—if men as well as women could "mother" children —then we might vanquish gender. Men and women would still have a few distinct body parts, of course, but "masculine" and "feminine" personality differences would no longer have anything to do with bodily equipment. No one would assume that only people with a certain kind of body should be caring and empathic. The speed with which a child became independent would no longer depend on whether it was male or female. A new era would dawn.

Yet even if this understanding of gender as learned behavior is right, androgyny proponents quickly run into a problem. As Chodorow herself underscores, mothering by women produces women who themselves want to be mothers. The mechanism at work may be social and psychological, rather than biological, but it's no less real for that. How, then, do you get women to mother less and men to mother more, especially when, according to Chodorow, everything in a typical male's early rearing makes him wrong for the job?

100

Plato faced this dilemma when he drew up history's first great plan for a perfectly just society in the Republic—a society that required, among other things, androgyny. His solution: send the members of the old, imperfect city into exile, so that the new, just city could be built from scratch. Otherwise, their recalcitrant mental habits would sabotage the creation of the new order. The fact is, attempts to force a society out of its most deeply held cultural values can be every bit as tyrannical as schemes to override our biological nature.

The kibbutzniks were utopian socialists who wanted to construct a society where the ideal of "from each according to his ability, to each according to his needs" would govern the production and distribution of goods. It was as part of this larger socialist vision that the kibbutzniks set out to wipe away gender.

Kibbutz parents agreed to see their own children only two hours a day, and for the remaining 22 hours to surrender them to the collective, which would raise them androgynously (trying more to "masculinize" women than "feminize" men). Boys and girls would henceforth do the same kind of work and wear the same kind of clothes. Girls would learn to be soldiers, just like boys. Signs of "bourgeois" femininity—makeup, say—would now be taboo. As if they had stepped out of Plato's Republic, the children would dress and undress together and even use the same showers.

The experiment collapsed within a generation, and a traditional family and gender system reasserted itself. Why? Those who believe in hardwired natural differences obviously would say that cultural conditioning couldn't remove the sexes' genetic programming. Indeed, in his now-infamous conference remarks, Lawrence Summers invoked the history of the kibbutz movement to help make his case that biology might partially explain sex roles.

Feminists, though, say that the kibbutz experiment didn't get a fair chance. However committed to gender justice the kibbutzniks might have been, they were all traditional Europeans by upbringing. Somehow they must have transmitted the old cultural messages about gender to the children. Perhaps, too, those messages came from the larger Israeli society, from which it was impossible to shelter the boys and girls entirely. What's more—and Chodorow would doubtless emphasize this fact—the kibbutz child-care nurses were all women. A 50/50 male-female mix might have done the trick.

Yet American androgyny proponents rarely refer to the kibbutz experiment—for understandable reasons. Its failure—even if you accept their own cultural explanation for it—puts a serious damper on the idea of androgynizing America. In the U.S., after all, there's nothing remotely approaching the level of commitment to surmounting gender found among the early kibbutzniks. If androgyny proved unattainable in a small socialist society whose citizens self-selected for radical feminist convictions, how could one bring it about in contemporary America, where most people don't want it? It would take a massive amount of coercion—unacceptable in any democracy —to get us even to the point where the kibbutzniks were when they failed to build a post-gender society.

The best account of the experiment's breakdown, offered by anthropologist Melford Spiro in his books Gender and Culture and Children of the Kibbutz, points out an even bigger obstacle to androgyny. Ultimately, Spiro argues, the kibbutzniks didn't succeed because the mothers wanted their kids back. They wanted to take care of their young children in the old-fashioned way, themselves. Two hours a day with their kids wasn't enough. Even among the kibbutz founders, Spiro notes, women often agonized over the sacrifice of maternal pleasure that their egalitarian ideology demanded. He quotes from one mother's autobiography: "Is it right to make the child return for the night to the children's home, to say goodnight to it and send it back to sleep among the fifteen or twenty others? This parting from the child before sleep is so unjust!" Such feelings persisted and intensified, until collective pressure forced the kibbutz to let parents spend extra time with their kids.

True, the last 40 years have seen tremendous changes in the social roles of men and women—changes that could never have happened were there not significant flexibility in gender roles. From the standpoint of feminism's ideal of androgyny, though, the shift is still very partial. Until the link between women and child rearing completely breaks down, neither corporate boardrooms nor Harvard professorships of mathematics will see numerical parity between men and women. In the meantime, in disproportionate numbers, at critical points in their careers, women will continue to choose mothering over

9.5 Positive and negative androgyny and their relationship with psychological health and well-being

Traditional androgyny is seen as a gender role identity that consists of a balance of positive feminine and positive masculine traits. Androgyny is thought to be a balanced identity that combines the virtues of both genders. However, gender stereotypes do not include only desirable aspects of femininity and masculinity (Kelly & Worrell, 1977; Ricciardelli & Williams, 1995). Socially undesirable feminine and masculine traits are also important to gender stereotypes and may even be dominant (Spence et al., 1979). **Logically then, an androgynous gender role identity may also consist of a balance of negative feminine and negative masculine traits, that is, an identity that combines the failings/defects of both genders and thus creates the possibility of an undesirable or negatively androgynous gender role identity. The presence of significant levels of negative feminine and negative masculine traits in androgynous individuals may have a detrimental effect on the androgynous gender role identity to the extent that such negative behaviors may override any of the positive benefits proposed for the androgynous person** (Woodhill & Samuels, in press).

9.6 From a poll to Transsexuals concerning belief or acceptance of Androgynes as a Gender Identity

Do FtM's & MtF's think androgynes are wierd or crazy?

48.8%   Believes or somewhat believes that Androgyne is a valid Gender Identity

40.8%   Does not believe that Androgyne is a valid Gender Identity

10.3%   Is undecided or unsure

9.7 Magical Thinking, Extreme Ego-Defense and Sociopathic Behaviour[xxxii]

Fact: Not one of the neurological based studies have shown any evidence that there is a "middle ground" in neurology. Quite to the contrary the evidence all points right now to either/or instead.

The scientific evidence thus far all points to one simple conclusion. Someone with a female central nervous system will eventually reject having male anatomy. What this means practically is some classically transsexed individuals might fight off this end point, but eventually they will get there. This is the well documented dsyphoric imperative leading to the eventual "GID crisis" that forces one to change or die or go stark raving mad. There is no middle ground in this except as a temporary measure and there is absolutely no evidence thus far to back claims of a "half gender" neurology, insisting that will be discovered is magical thinking and ego defensive until ANY evidence is uncovered supporting it. Using such magical thinking to justify the partial and extreme sociopathic reactions is evidence of mental illness. This is what the most extreme of the transvestite/transgender crowd does and it is past time mental health professionals stop apologizing for them and use a sociopathic model to see what is going on.

Chapter 10 Why are names important?[xxxiii]

First names can be important because they are normally given by parents making a conscious decision. It is important because the name is how the person might be named for the rest of their lives, unless changed in the future. Names are normally given after much thought and exploring feelings. Sometimes names are used over-and-over in a family. Sometimes names are picked from desired virtues and characteristics. Nicknames can also be used and is a factor in being named. Someone from a foreign country my change their name to the new countries style of name, similar sounding to their original names. Sometimes names are picked out of popular names, or the opposite unique names.

Gender neutral names

Names can be restrictive in that many names "assign" gendered behavior, appearance, and genitals. If I say the name "Barbie", what comes to your mind, or "Abraham"?

So many non-binary gendered person choose to rename themselves with unisex, non-gender specific , androgynous, gender neutral names. What comes to your mind when you hear the names "Jordan", "Pat", "Jessie", or "Jamie"?

In renaming, they normally try to base the name off of their original names somewhat, either directly or indirectly.

Gendered "sides" names

Sometimes bigendered, crossdressers, and those with hidden, multiple, or separate parts of their lives choose to go with names for the different sides of their lives. Masculine, feminine, neutral, mixed, or unusual names are common in non-binary gender.

Of course this is not something new. Many cisgendered people have "family", friend, or coworker nicknames, separate from legal "real" names.

Online names

Going online and participating in groups, forums, and blogs can lead to having online virtual names. These are names that one does not use in real everyday life, rather just for group participation as usernames. Sometimes names to protect one's identity, to remain anonymous are used.

Unisex Name List

Much has been written about male or masculine, and female or feminine names. So I will focus rather on gender neutral or unisex names.

You can consult online or several books that list unisex/gender neutral names.

Gender Neutral Names from the US Census with ranked of popularity.

Abby – 694 (related to Abigail and Abraham)

Alexis – 457 , Alex - 2660

(Alexandra- 396, Alexandria-f 747, Alexa-f 1227, Alexia-f 1818, Alexander-f 2170

Ali – 2434 (related to Aliyah-f, Alison, Alistair, Alexander, and Alicia)

Angel - 424   (related to Angela-f 29, Angelica-f 390, Angelina- f414, Angeline-f 650, Angelia-f 658,

       Angelita-f 943,Angelique-f 965, Angelia-f 1948, Angelika-f 2465)

Ariel – 1113 (related to Arielle-f 1888)

Ashton – 1681, Ash (related to names that start with Ash~)

Avery – 3227 (related to Freda f and Alfred)

Bailey – 1836

Billie – (related to Bill, Will, William, Wilma, Liam, Guillermo)

Blair – 1356f 748m

Bo -

Bobby – 1019, Robin – 100, Bobbie (related to Bobbie, Bobbi, Robert, Roberta, Robyn, Rob, and   Robby)

Cameron - 1862

Casey – 461, Kasey - 847)(related to Kacey-f 1893)

Christian(a) – 903, Chris- 528, Kris- 833 (related to Christine-f 43, Christina-f 70, Christy-f 260,

       Christie-f 431)

Dakota - 4077

Devin – 1606 , Devon - 1154

Dominique - 672

Drew – 3273, (related to Andy, Andrea, Andre, and Andrew)

Jaime - 1643

Jamie - 146

Jessie - 215

Jordan - 792

Kendall - 1514

Logan - 3553

Micah - 2413

Morgan - 576
Payton -
Quinn - 3691
Reagan - 3202
Ryan - 1229
Sage - 3769
Shannon - 123
Shea - 2270
Sidney - 1483
Taylor - 805
Tyler - 2663

A more complete list can be found in Wikipedia. See "Unisex names" for a list of names. http://en.wikipedia.org/wiki/Unisex_names

Gender Neutral Pronouns
This section concerns US English (which in this writing I will just write
"English") only. It may also apply to the other English (UK, Canada,
Australia, Indian, etc) however, at this moment the author has no knowledge
of such area. Each language and sometimes the individual dialects, have their
own individual (many times sharing similar language features) structures,
rules, semantics, and grammar.

Gender connection
Gender and gender identity affects English (and probably most other
languages. The last chapter dealt with one part of speech, the noun. A
person's name as mentioned last chapter can denote gender, gender
expression, and gender expectations. After nouns, or more important to those
happy with their names, pronouns may affect one experiencing gender
identity disorders or concerns.

When I say, "There she is over there," what comes to your mind? Probably
that the person someone is looking for is located within sight, and the gender
is feminine and maybe even the sex that person located is female.
Transgender crossdressers and drag performers may or may not refer to each
other using opposite their sex pronouns when dressed up, depending on one's
personal preference.

The business world made great strides in becoming more gender neutral in
the workplace. One attending school in the last decade would recognize the
importance of gender neutrality, mostly caused by the increase in female
population in higher paid corporate positions compared to the decades
proceeding.

Emergence of Gender Neutral Pronouns[xxxiv]
To those not in the gender (and sometimes sexual biological) binary,
pronouns can become a crutch, anchor, curse, limitation, and annoyance.

Modern accepted English allows for a few ways to avoid the gendering of
pronouns. Many use a mixture of methods.
  • "He or she" and "his or her" - its fairly common to hear these words
    in everyday speech now days. Although not androgynous and still
    denoting a binary, it does create a gender ambiguity that gender
    sensitive individuals may find more accepting, and may relieve a little
    more tension without causing tension among the non-androgynous
    speaking people. This is also related to the written form of "(s)he" or

"s/he." The limits of doing this also are in that using it can make speaking a little more long-winded and formal.

- "She" some more feminist have resorted to using she instead of he when gender is unspecified and general. Doing so certainly changes the tone and is noticeable especially at heavily mixed gender groupings and organizations.
- Singular "they, their, them, em (commonly spoken)". Using this is acceptable except among some that believe that doing so is ungrammatical. Doing so avoids specifying a gender and also has a benefit of fitting well with those multi-gender. The use of "we" may be used by plural-gender to refer to a singular bodied person with several genders and identities. More often they refer to each gender with it's own name and desired gender pronoun.
- Use their names (first or last) sparingly. Using the last name without a gender title, can sound informal and avoids repeating the first name. Nicknames also can be used to add more variety in informal situations.
- "One" is also a great word when speaking in general concerning something specific. It is a crafty way of taking someone specific, and then speaking about them in a general manner, put still enabling one to comment or say something about that specific person. Using "one" is especially good when giving advice.
- Avoid "mam" and "sir" if possible. For the most part, they are unnecessary.

Modern English Pronoun Chart

			subjective	objective	reflexive
				personal pronoun	
first-person	singular		I	me	myself
	plural		we	us	ourselves *ourself*
second-person	singular	standard (archaic formal)	you, *ya* (IPA: /jə/)	you, *ya* (IPA: /jə/)	yourself
		archaic informal	*thou*	*thee*	*thyself*
	plural	standard	you, *ya* (IPA: /jə/)	you, *ya* (IPA: /jə/)	yourselves
		archaic	*ye*	*you*	*yourselves*
		nonstandard	*you guys*	*you guys*	*yourselves y'all's selves*
			you all y'all	*you gals you all*	
			youse youse guys	*y'all youse*	
			youse gals	*youse guys*	
			you-uns	*youse gals*	

you-uns
yous

yis
yinz
you lot

		Nominative	Accusative	Reflexive	Possessive
singular	**masculine**	he	him	himself	his
	feminine	she	her	herself	hers
	neuter	it	it	itself	-
third-person	**generic/epicene (formal)**	one	one	oneself	-
	generic/epicene (nonstandard)	*they*	*them*	*themself, themselves*	*theirs*
	plural	they	them, *'em* (IPA: /əm/)	themselves	theirs

Which **Old English** looked somewhat different.

Old English personal pronouns

			Nominative pron.		Accusative	Dative	Genitive
1st		**Singular**	iċ	[ɪtʃ]	me(c)	me	min
		Dual	wit	[wɪt]	unc		uncer
		Plural	wé	[weː]	us		ure
2nd		**Singular**	þū	[θuː]	þe		þin
		Dual	ġit	[jɪt]	inc		incer
		Plural	ġē	[jeː]	eow		eower his
3rd	**Singular**	**Masculine**	hē	[heː]	hine	him	his
		Neuter	hit	[hɪt]	hit	him	
		Feminine	hēo	[heːo]	hie	hire	hire
	Plural		hīe	[hiːə]	hie	him	hira

Nominative became subjective. Accusative (direct object) and dative (indirect object) merged. Genitive became possessive.

The pronoun *hit* is the word where *it* comes from.

Here is Wikipedia's current list of some **gender neutral pronouns**.

	Nominative (subject)	Accusative (object)	Possessive adjective	Possessive pronoun
He	*He* laughed	I called *him*	*His* eyes gleam	That is *his*
She	*She* laughed	I called *her*	*Her* eyes gleam	That is *hers*
It	*It* laughed	I called *it*	*Its* eyes gleam	That is *its*
One	*One* laughed	I called *one*	*One's* eyes gleam	That is *one's*
Singular *they*	*They* laughed	I called *them*	*Their* eyes gleam	That is *theirs*

Co	*Co* laughed	I called *co*	*Cos* eyes gleam	That is *cos*
Spivak (new)	*Ey* laughed	I called *em*	*Eir* eyes gleam	That is *eirs*
Spivak (old)	*E* laughed	I called *em*	*Eir* eyes gleam	That is *eirs*
S/he	*S/he* laughed	I called *him/her*	*His/her* eyes gleam	That is *his/hers*
Sie and hir[*citation needed*]	*Sie* laughed	I called *hir*	*Hir* eyes gleam	That is *hirs*
Xe[7]	*Xe* laughed	I called *xem*	*Xyr* eyes gleam	That is *xyrs*
Ve[8]	*Ve* laughed	I called *ver*	*Vis* eyes gleam	That is *vis*
Ze and mer[9]	*Ze* laughed	I called *mer*	*Zer* eyes gleam	That is *zer*
Ze (or zie) and hir[10]	*Ze* laughed	I called *hir*	*Hir* eyes gleam	That is *hirs*
Tey[*citation needed*]	*Tey* /teɪ/ laughed	I called *tem* /təm/	*Tes* /təz/ eyes gleam	That is *tes* /tɛz/
Zie[*citation needed*]	*Zie* laughed	I called *zir*	*Zir* eyes gleam	That is *zirs*
E[*citation needed*]	*E* laughed	I called *het*	*Het* eyes gleam	That is *hets*
En[*citation needed*]	*En* laughed	I called *en*	*Ens* eyes gleam	That is *ens*
Thon[11]	*Thon* laughed	I called *thon*	*Thons* eyes gleam	That is *thon's*
Shey[*citation needed*]	*Shey* laughed	I called *shem*	*Shis* eyes gleam	That is *shis*
'E[*citation needed*]	*'E* laughed	I called *h'*	*'S* eyes gleam	That is *'s*
Squee and squir[*citation needed*]	*Squee* laughed	I called *squir*	*Squir* eyes gleam	That is *squirs*
Quee and queer[*citation needed*]	*quee* laughed	I called *queer*	*Queers* eyes gleam	That is *queer's*

Further issues and concerns of Non-binary gender.

1.) Better informed psychologists, social workers, and psychiatrists. Possibly create a list of non-binary (not just TG or TS) friendly professionals for referrals.

2.) Further medical and scientific research concerning non-binary (and multiple) gender. Possibly recruit or advertise someway of getting these professionals interested in pursuing such research or studies, yet without bias.

3.) Legal, workplace, and political protection for various countries. Focus on facing, helping, reducing, or eliminating discrimination, violence, and barriers of service.

   1. List organizes that currently provide such services.
   2. List events and community building actions

4.) Access to medical, insurance, HRT, surgery, and plastic surgery in accordance to legal and ethical guidelines. Possibly create a list of non-binary friendly professionals for such service.

   1. Publishing possible successful legal processes needed to attain services.

5.) Exploring of non-binary gender love relationship information. Maybe a list of dating services that cater to non-binary gender persons, or creation of such services, so that such persons could have a secured, trusting, and confidential place to meet such like minded, or compatible persons.

6.) Publish more easy to use non-binary "coming out" type information so that revealing one's identity is simplified.

7.) Figure out a way to "speak" in understandable terms. Non-binary gender terminology is sometimes vague, limited, inconsistent, and non-specific.

Chapter 13 History

As one who has only recently the past few years discovered the community of Androgyne, Genderqueer, and Non-Binary Gender community on the Internet, I took advantage of all the information and experiences inherited from earlier generations. So first and foremost I would like to recognize only some of the inspirations or sources of such things, in a modern time line, beginning in the early 90s. At the same time, I will introduce some of the Non-Binary Gender terms and identities.

13.1 A history of Non-Binary Gender (1991 to 2008)

I am sure the history goes well before this time period of almost two decades, and there is much I have missed that is inclusive during this time period. Much of which history probably exists pre-Internet era. But such history is unknown to the author at this time. Such history would be tackled better by a transgender or Androgyne historian. And would be great information for a book, thesis, or website itself.

Having said the limits of such history, no access to libraries of gender identity related material, I will say that it is the first attempt at an exclusively focused non-binary gender timeline that I have seen, anywhere. Although you will see the Cyborg Manifesto and Kate Bornstein's books on other transgender histories and timelines, the rest is unique to non-binary genderism, and I believe you will see this first here.

Post-Gender (1991)
Post-Gender first discussed in Donna Haraway http://en.wikipedia.org/wiki/Donna_Haraway
"A Cyborg Manifesto: Science, Technology, and Socialist-Feminism in the Late Twentieth Century," in 1991.
http://www.stanford.edu/dept/HPS/Haraway/CyborgManifesto.html

A modern summary of Postgenderism essence can be found at IEEC, in the abstract of one of the papers titled,"Postgenderism: Beyond the Gender Binary (IEET White Paper 03)" By George Dvorsky and James Hughes, PhD.3/20/2008

> IEET Postgenderism: Beyond the Gender Binary (IEET White Paper 03)
> http://ieet.org/index.php/IEET/category/C111/
> Postgenderism is an extrapolation of ways that technology is eroding the biological, psychological and social role of gender, and an

argument for why the erosion of binary gender will be liberatory. Postgenderists argue that gender is an arbitrary and unnecessary limitation on human potential, and foresee the elimination of   115 involuntary biological and psychological gendering in the human species through the application of neurotechnology, biotechnology and reproductive technologies. Postgenderists contend that dyadic gender roles and sexual dimorphisms are generally to the detriment of individuals and society. Assisted reproduction will make it possible for individuals of any sex to reproduce in any combinations they choose, with or without "mothers" and "fathers," and artificial wombs will make biological wombs unnecessary for reproduction. Greater biological fluidity and psychological androgyny will allow future persons to explore both masculine and feminine aspects of personality. Postgenderists do not call for the end of all gender traits, or universal androgyny, but rather that those traits become a matter of choice. Bodies and personalities in our postgender future will no longer be constrained and circumscribed by gendered traits, but enriched by their use in the palette of diverse self-expression.

Gender Outlaw
(1994, 1995) Kate Bornstein
Gender Ambiguity and Gender Fluidity. Gender Outlaw. Although not exclusively non-binary gender focused, there is some good basic information mixed in the book.

Androgyny RAQ (Rarely Asked Questions)
(1994-2002)

Last modified: 21 March 1998 by Raphael Carter

Raphael Carter is a science fiction writer.
http://en.wikipedia.org/wiki/Raphael_Carter

Contains a basic dictionary, guide to androgynous behavior (manners), reading list, reviews, and gender concepts. Gender Outlaws by Bornstein is listed as a reference.

Carter who Also made:

The Angel's Dictionary
Last modified: 14 July 1996 by Raphael Carter
http://web.archive.org/web/20041204191835/www.chaparraltree.com/raq/angels.shtml

This dictionary list has this definitions of androgyne , genderfuck, and gender outlaw(see later this chapter concerning meanings of Androgyne). It also has some terms which aren't used as much now day such as Epicene, which Raphael later identifies with more than Androgyne.

Gender Anarchoterrosism
(1997)
Gender Anarchoterrorism 101
1997, Mikhail Pokrovscky
http://www.geocities.com/WestHollywood/Heights/2011/gender.html

Genderqueer
(1997)
I see a few references to Genderqueer.

Era of Listservs, Webrings, and Newsgroups
Sphere
Created December 11, 1997
http://web.archive.org/web/20030621061019/http://www.devrandom.net/~aidan/sphere.html
Sphere appears to be the first real grouping of non-binary gendered persons exclusively. From the description of the group you can see where the focus was back then.

> Sphere is a listserv for people who bend even the boundaries of transgenderism. It's a bunch of people who identify as both genders, or no gender, or third-gendered... I'm trying to think if I forgot any possibilities :-) We'll share what it's like to be queerer than queer, discuss how we fit into trans and other communities, fight the good activist fight, and tell cool stories about our genderfucked experiences.

> We take our name from the idea that gender isn't a dichotomy (where there's either male or female) or a continuum (where there's a rainbow of stuff in between, all in a line and all related to male or female) but a sphere, where male and female are just two of an infinite number of possible points and you can be anywhere on, inside, or outside, the gendered world.

116

My Gender Workbook: How to Become a Real Man, a Real Woman, the Real You, or Something Else Entirely
January 19, 1998 Kate Bornstein
This jewel of a book is packed with stuff to make one ponder, presented in a fun and active way.

Intergendered
(1998)
What Is Intergendered? By: Donna Lynn Matthews. October 1998
http://cydathria.com/ms_donna/intergen.html
Intergendered is a gendered state between the polar endpoints of man and
woman. It amounts to a wholesale rejection of the binary gender system and
declaring that there is more than just man or woman. It comes down to
stating that there are as many valid gendered states as there are people. Some
may feel strong (or weak) masculine and feminine qualities all at the same
time. Some may not see themselves on the gender spectrum at all, describing
what amounts to a null gendered state.

Intergender Webring
03/25/1999 http://www.webring.com/t/Intergender
Within the transgendered community, there is a growing subgroup who do
not identify as either a 'man' or 'woman', but as somewhere inbetween. In
some cases, they identify as neither, placing themselves 'outside' of the
gender 'spectrum' completely.

The Webring of Androgyny
Community Created 01/27/2000
Androgyn Art & Writing:. (T-Diaries) - - - - - - - - - - - - - - - A ring for
Androgyn, transsexual & transgendered sites that have diaries, rants, poetry
or even art. Any site that deals with gender issues are welcome.

Genderqueer Edition of FORGE Newsletter
5/12/2000
This document is good at showing some of the information available before
the year 2000, many of which I have listed in this list.
http://www.forge-forward.org/newsletters/pdf/200005-GQ-Spirit-SM-
news.pdf

13.2 Androgyne (Orig-1994-1996-1998-2000)
Androgyne- original meaning, hermaphrodite
According to dictionary.com the origin of the word , an·dro·gyne /ˈændrə
ˌdʒaɪn/ an-druh-jahynis, is 1545–55 an Old French word. This word comes
from the Latin word androgynus. The latin word comes from the Greek word
andrógynos, which all means hermaphrodite. The Greek word is made up of
three root words which are andro-, gyn-, and -os (masc. n. suffix) [xxxv]

Andro is from Greek andró(s), meaning man.[xxxvi] Gyn is from Greek, which is
a form of gynaik-, which means female or woman. [xxxvii]

So Andro+Gyne means man-woman, male-female, or as it was used up till modern time in English, hermaphrodite. Androgyne still is the word used for hermaphrodite in the French language.

The most popular definition in most major dictionaries (Webster, American Heritage, Oxford) is Hermaphrodite.[xxxviii] It can also apply to plant life dual sex. Sometimes it refers to a divine godly dual natured being, or the unity to the divine. Some broad online dictionaries are starting to add the androgynous person and some gender identity references. Most TG dictionaries define it as both or neither male or female, a gender identity. Some times it means mixed gender (both), sometimes excluding the agender (neither). It all depends on the context used[xxxix].

The kind of androgyne we are talking about here in this book refers to gender identity. Androgyne as a gender identity isn't in any of the major dictionaries, Marriam-Webster and American Heritage (which defines androgyne as a hermaphrodite), yet.

Marian Rothstein writes about how the word was used Renaissance writers made use of the androgyne as a figure of desire (both heterosexual and homosexual), of marital fidelity and marital infidelity, and of the soul seeking union with the divine.[xl]

Earliest modern source of use of Androgyne as a gender identity that I could find is 1994 to 1996 according to sources shows Raphael Carter's websites listed above (see the Androgyny RAQ and Angel's Dictionary).

There are four references to Androgyne in Kate Bornstein's My Gender Workbook: How to Become a Real Man, a Real Woman, the Real You, or Something Else Entirely

Era of Groups, Live Journals, and Forums

First Gender Identity use of Androgyne's in a Group (2000)
Founded: Dec 18, 2000
androgynes · Living beyond gender Yahoo Group,
http://groups.yahoo.com/group/androgynes/

4/20/01
Androgyne Online by Stephe Feldman

8/11/01
genderoutlaws' Journal :Live Journal
http://community.livejournal.com/genderoutlaws/profile

3/4/2002
The Genderqueer Community: Live Journal
http://community.livejournal.com/genderqueer/

8/2002
Genderqueer: Voices from beyond the sexual binary
August 2002 published by Joan Nestle, Clare Howell, and Riki
Wilchins. Published by Alison Books.

11/13/2002
Poly-Gendered People's Journal: Live Journal
http://community.livejournal.com/polygender_ppl/profile

Androgynes: Live Journal
27 Jul 2003
http://community.livejournal.com/androgynes/profile

Androgyne Forum at Susans.org(formerly Genderqueer)
June 03, 2005
http://www.susans.org/forums/index.php/board,57.0.html

Androgyne Within
June 11th, 2006
http://community.livejournal.com/androgynewithin/profile

What Is Gender? Forum
November, 2007
http://www.whatisgender.net
A support forum for transgendered, non_binary, and significant others.

Relationships
If men are from Mars, women are from Venus, does that mean non-binary gender persons are from Earth?

I write this chapter with hesitancy. My major issue isn't the importance of non-binary gender relationships, rather the inexperience and knowledge of "successful" information. Therefore this chapter may rely on theory studies, and some guesswork. Hopefully one day such a chapter will exist more reliable and informative.

Very little information is available concerning non-binary gender relationships compared to gay, lesbian, crossdresser, and even transsexual.

The author's own personal relationship and past relationships may be the source of such hesitancy.

Fear of relationships
Especially problematic is the fear that non-binary gender persons have of problems arising in a relationship because of their gender identity. This was rated as the second most common fear.

Possible sources of fears
For existing relationships that one may "come out" in, such changes could sign the end of the relationship.

For those entering new relationships, yet already knowing their gender identity, what one reveals to the new partner becomes an issue.

For others that reveal fully their gender identity, other issues become prominent.

Theoretical formula for Successful Relationship
Theoretically speaking, a relationship where one *reveals fully* their gender identity, current and/or desire sex anatomy, current and/or future gender expressions, that was, has become, or continues to be consistent, reliable, and stable, and still maintains mutual attraction, passion, commitment, intimacy, and commitment are in the best position for success. Finding such relationship, is another story, unless you already happen to be one of these lucky persons.

A good place to start any discussion on relationships is with current theory of

love, attraction, and orientations.
[http://faculty.plattsburgh.edu/alan.marks/Soc%20361/CHAPTER %208%20LOVE%20AND%20ROMANTIC%20RELATIONSHIPS.htm]

Love = Intimacy + Passion + Decision/commitment

Intimacy is the closeness, connectivity, and bonding shared between two people that are friends.
> Types of intimacy: physical, emotional, intellectual and spiritual. Openness, can talk about anything, honesty, understanding, trust, forgiveness, sharing, respect
> [http://dating.about.com/od/glossarywordsijk/g/intimacy.htm]

> Elements of Intimacy
> 1. Desire the happiness of that person.
> 2. Mutual understanding
> 3. Be able to count on that person.
> 4. Give and receive emotional support.

Passion is an intense emotion that gives rise to compelling feelings, enthusiasm, or desire for someone, leading towards romance, physical attraction, and sexual feelings. Euphoria, physiological arousal, sexual attraction, Energy

Decision/commitment in the short term the decision that one loves someone and in the long term, the commitment to maintain that love. It includes cognitive elements in decision making. Devotion, Commitment, Protectiveness, Loyalty, Security

> memory, association, concept formation, language, attention, perception, action, problem solving and mental imagery.

Attraction = Interest + Rapport and Connection

Appendix: Poll that deals with several issues, taken by 10 people born male.[xli]

Poll A

Question

How do you feel about your gender? (Tick all choices that apply to you.)

Responses

Choices		Votes
I was born female	0	
I was born intersexed	2	
If a magic wand could change my sex, I would do it	9	
If men could wear whatever they want, I would have very few gender problems left	7	
My body conforms to my birth sex	6	
My body does not completely conform to my birth sex	3	
My body does not conform at all to my birth sex	1	
I am (mostly) asexual	3	
I am homosexual (towards people of my birth sex)	0	
I am heterosexual (towards people other than my birth sex)	5	
I am bisexual	3	
I have an S.O. with whom I live	7	
I date someone, but do not live with anyone	0	
I don't even date anyone	4	
I have been mistaken as the other sex (related to birth sex)	4	
I am transitioning to the other sex	1	
I have taken hormones	3	
I have seriously comtemplated with the idea of changing my sex	4	
More than 50% of time, I wear items that are usually only worn by the other sex	10	
I have serious problems with my S.O. regarding what I wish to wear	3	
I have serious problems in my job regarding what I wish to wear	5	
I have serious problems with my friends regarding what I wish to wear	3	
I sometimes think that the only way out of my misery is a suicide	1	
I have found that my androgyny is, sometimes at least, a blessing to me	10	
I was born male	10	

124 **Poll B**

Question

Questions about sex, androgyny and religion. [xlii]
Responses

Choices	Votes
I was born male (androgynes included)	12
I was born female (androgynes included)	4
I was born intersexual (only physically intersexed)	0
I am (or becoming) a full-time androgyne	9
I intend to become a full-time androgyne	1
I would like to be a full-time androgyne but cannot	4
Part-time androgyny suits me well	2
Looking androgynous is not my thing	2
I am transitioning to be the other sex	1
I am an atheist	1
I am agnostic	1
I am mainstream Christian	1
I am another type of Christian	1
My religion is an established mainstream world religion (jewish, islam, buddhism, hinduism, taoism, shintoism, etc)	3
I am a neopagan (wicca, druidism, asatru, ...)	3
My religion is something else	7
My sexuality is mainstream	4
I like S&M things (broadly understood)	0
I have sexual fetishes (at least one)	7
I am a sexual voyer (affects your behaviour)	2
I am a sexual exhibitionist (have done it in real life)	2
I am socially asexual (not affecting social life)	6
I am functionally asexual (no interest or nonfunctional)	3
I have some other special issues in sexuality	3

Question

How are you feel you are usually perceived in your daily life interacting with society in general?[xliii]

Responses

Choices	Votes	% 1 reply
As a male	42	57
As a women	15	20
As an androgynous person	16	21

Poll D

Question

Based on recent discussions I was wondering as androgynes if our heights were skewed from the traditional shorter females & taller males such as more shorter birth males & taller birth females? Please pick birth sex & closest height combination![xliv]

Responses

Choices	Votes	% 1 reply	Respondents
Male below 5 foot	0	0	
Female below 5 foot	1	2	silverrainweb@...
Male from 5' 0" - 5' 2"	0	0	
Female from 5' 0" - 5' 2"	1	2	entitything@...
Male from 5' 3" - 5' 5"	4	9	normpdx@... aenneapdx@... finally_tina@... steve_freereeder@...
Female from 5' 3" - 5' 5"	3	6	darkoshi7@... capeboy_lego@... emilycurewitz2@...
Male from 5' 6" - 5' 8"	8	18	mrwooloo@... lev_tools@... ilaria1111@... xino@... verdantseek@... punkinnk@... alex4022@... madonis_@...
Female from 5' 6" - 5' 8"	1	2	janeiebliss@...
Male from 5' 9" - 5' 11"	10	23	christina.marsland@... janicegordon2002@... redoblk@... scfeldman@... xiomberg@... SoniaAzul@... alynna@... terrileetg@... ajcoles@... celtic-laura@...
Female from 5' 9" - 5' 11"	1	2	LHNorton@...

Do you believe in a binary gender system.[xlv]

Yes, Of course.	8.59 % (14)
No, gender is not real.	12.27 % (20)
There are three or more genders.	73.62 % (120)
What does binary mean?	5.52 % (9)

Total votes: 163

Androgynes, Genderqueer, Non-Binary Gender Variants

Total populations:

USA Androgynes **118,665** to **237, 422**

UK - 60,943,912[xlvi] (July 2008 est.) 23,704 to 47,427
Canada – 33,424,260[xlvii] (Nov 9, 2008 est.) 13,000 to 26,011
Australia – 21,481,389[xlviii] (Nov 10, 2008 est.) 8,355 to 16,717

Estimated world population: **2,600,000** and **5,200,000** world Non-Binary Gendered (Androgynes, Genderqueers, etc).

Biological Sex:	USA	UK	Canada	Australia	World
Male-bodied:	88,239 to 176,547	17,626 to 35,267	9,667 to 19,342	6,212 to 12,431	1,933,360 to 3,866,720
Female-bodied:	26,878 to 53,776	5,369 to 10,742	2,945 to 5,891	1,892 to 3,786	588,900 to 1,177,800
Intersex-bodied:	4,331 to 8,666	865 to 1,731	475 to 949	304 to 610	94,900 to 189,800

Gender Subdivision:	USA	UK	Canada	Australia	World
Mixed, Both, Androgyne, some Genderqueers, Intergender, Ambigender	47,462 to 94,924	9,482 to 18,964	5,200 to 10,404	3,342 to 6,687	1,040,000 to 2,080,000
Neither, Agender, Null Gender, Genderless, Neutrois	17,800 to 35,613	3,556 to 7,114	1,950 to 3,902	1,253 to 2,508	173k to 346k
Self-Defined and Unlabeled Genders, Postgender (and a bunch of other labels unique)	17,800 to 35,613	3,556 to 7,114	1,950 to 3,902	1,253 to 2,508	173k to 346k
Undecided, Bigender	11,867 to 23,742	2,370 to 4,743	1.3k to 2.6k	835 to 1.7k	260k to 520k
Fluid	6k-12k	1k-2k	.5k-1k	.5k-1k	~200k

i Levels of GID for Androgynes, Bi-gendered, etc. by Zythyra (aka y2gender)
Retrieved September 05, 2008, from Susans.org
http://www.susans.org/forums/index.php/topic,17905.0.html

ii Would You Say You Were Scatterbrained [Poll] by Pica Pica. Retrieved September
11, 2008, from Susans.org.
http://www.susans.org/forums/index.php/topic,16165.0.html

iii How lazy or active are you? (physically, activity, socially, goals, dreams) [Poll].
Retrieved September 11, 2008, from Susans.org.
http://www.susans.org/forums/index.php/topic,19236.0.html

ivHow good is your self esteem? [Poll]. Retrieved September 11, 2008 from
Susans.org. http://www.susans.org/forums/index.php/topic,16161.0.html
vTG Education: TS exclusion of CD/TV/Non-Binary/Bigender by Kendall on Sun Jul
13, 2008 http://www.whatisgender.net/phpBB3/viewtopic.php?f=137&t=1231

viAnyone have a list or link to page with a reading list by Kendall on Tue Jul 15, 2008

vii androgyne. (n.d.). *Dictionary.com Unabridged (v 1.1)*. Retrieved September 05,
2008, from Dictionary.com website: http://dictionary.reference.com/browse/androgyne

vii Sex chromosome illustration. http://www.genome.gov/glossary.cfm?key=sex
%20chromosomeThe sex chromosomes are the 23rdchromosome.

Viii A room of one's own 1929 http://ebooks.adelaide.edu.au/w/woolf/virginia/w9lr/

viii andro-. (n.d.). *Dictionary.com Unabridged (v 1.1)*. Retrieved September 05, 2008,
from Dictionary.com website: http://dictionary.reference.com/browse/andro-

ix gyneco-. (n.d.). *Dictionary.com Unabridged (v 1.1)*. Retrieved September 05, 2008,
from Dictionary.com website: http://dictionary.reference.com/browse/gyneco-

x androgyne. (n.d.). *Dictionary.com Unabridged (v 1.1)*. Retrieved September 05,
2008, from Dictionary.com website: http://dictionary.reference.com/browse/androgyne

xiSee discussion in the post concerning uses of Androgyne in the "Possible Preface to
an androgyne book" post at Whatisgender.net.
http://www.whatisgender.net/phpBB3/viewtopic.php?f=147&t=1373

xii From Abstract at CAT.INIST.FR Mutations of the androgyne: Its functions in early
modern French literature = Les mutations de l'androgyne : Ses fonctions dans la
littérature de la Renaissance website
http://cat.inist.fr/?aModele=afficheN&cpsidt=15102560

xiii gender identity. (n.d.). *Dictionary.com Unabridged (v 1.1)*. Retrieved September
05, 2008, from Dictionary.com website:
http://dictionary.reference.com/browse/gender identity

xiv Sexuality: Gender Identity. Retrieved September 06, 2008 from www.emedicine.com website http://www.emedicine.com/ped/TOPIC2789.HTM

xv gender role. (n.d.). *Webster's New Millennium™ Dictionary of English, Preview Edition*

[http://en.wikipedia.org/wiki/Gender_identity]

(v 0.9.7). Retrieved September 06, 2008, from Dictionary.com website: http://dictionary.reference.com/browse/gender role

i How Old are you (for androgynes) Poll. Retrieved October 21, 2008 from Susans.org. http://www.susans.org/forums/index.php/topic,18102.0.

ii Are you male-bodied or female-bodied? [Poll]. Retrieved September 13, 2008 from Susans.org http://www.susans.org/forums/index.php/topic,27095.0/viewResults.html

iii What is your sex? [Poll]. Retrieved September 13, 2008 from Androgynes Yahoo Group. http://groups.yahoo.com/group/androgynes/surveys?id=868985

iv What is your sex and gender? [Poll]. Retrieved September 13, 2008 from Androgynes Yahoo Group http://groups.yahoo.com/group/androgynes/surveys?id=1030047

v Thinking outside the Gender Binary [Poll]. Retrieved January 04, 2008 from Livejournal at http://www.livejournal.com/poll/?id=1260263.

vi As an androgyne do you feel the need to change your body [Poll]. Retrieved October 10, 2008 from Susans.org. http://www.susans.org/forums/index.php/topic,38308.0.html

vii What is your sexual orientation? (androgyes) Poll. Retrieved September 11, 2008 from Susans.org. http://www.susans.org/forums/index.php/topic,18335.0.html

viii Are you Asexual or Sexual? [Poll]. Retrieved September 13, 2008 from Androgynes Yahoo Group. http://groups.yahoo.com/group/androgynes/surveys?id=2083855

ix What is your sexual preference? (Click all that apply) [Poll]. Retrieved September 13, 2008 from Androgynes Yahoo Group http://groups.yahoo.com/group/androgynes/surveys?id=1030050

x How many people know you are an androgyne? [Poll]. Retrieved September 13, 2008 from Susans.org. http://www.susans.org/forums/index.php/topic,14737.0/viewResults

xi How comfortable you are with your gender identity? [Poll]. Retrieved September 13, 2008 from Androgynes Yahoo Group http://groups.yahoo.com/group/androgynes/surveys?id=1030052

xii http://ai.eecs.umich.edu/people/conway/TS/TS-II.html#anchor635615

xiii http://www.susans.org/forums/index.php/topic,2290.0.html

xiv Understanding Transgender Lives by Brett Genny Beemyn & Sue Rankin http://www.umass.edu/stonewall/uploads/listWidget/9002/Understanding%20Transgender%20Lives.pdf

xv http://www.census.gov/main/www/popclock.html

xvi UK Population Estimate. https://www.cia.gov/library/publications/the-world-factbook/print/uk.html

xvii Canada Population Clock. http://www.statcan.ca/english/edu/clock/population.htm

xviii Australia Population Clock. http://www.abs.gov.au/ausstats/abs%40.nsf/94713ad445ff1425ca25682000192af2/1647509ef7e25faaca2568a900154b63?OpenDocument

xix http://www.susans.org/forums/index.php/topic,14446.0.html

xx Understanding Transgender Lives by Brett Genny Beemyn & Sue Rankin http://www.umass.edu/stonewall/uploads/listWidget/9002/Understanding%20Transgender%20Lives.pdf

xxi My Gender Identity. Retrieved September 30, 2008 from IFGE.

xxii What's your gender identity? [Poll] retrieved Jan 08, 2009 from http://www.crossdresserheaven.com/a-transgender-rose-by-any-other-name/

xxiii What type of androgyne are you? [Poll]. Retrieved September 11, 2008 from Susans.org http://www.susans.org/forums/index.php/topic,7211.0.html

xxiv The Non-binary, gender identities [Poll]. Retrieved May 12, 2011 from Laura's Playground http://www.lauras-playground.com/forums/index.php?showtopic=2397

xxvClosed poll taken from Androgyne: A call to remember our spiritual legacy Yahoo Group found at http://groups.yahoo.com/group/ANDROGYNE/surveys?id=564082

xxviWhat we mean by gender is fluid or flexible?. Retrieved September 17, 2008 from WikiAnswers. http://wiki.answers.com/Q/What_we_mean_by_gender_is_fluid_or_flexible

xxviiWebsite Poll: What areas is, might, or will be important to you of a possible adrogynic influence? http://www.susans.org/forums/index.php/topic,14002.0/viewResults.html

xxviii behavior. (n.d.). *Dictionary.com Unabridged (v 1.1)*. Retrieved September 09, 2008, from Dictionary.com website: http://dictionary.reference.com/browse/behavior

xxix What makes you different from (most) people of your birth sex? [Poll] Retrieved September 13, 2008 from Androgynes Yahoo Group http://groups.yahoo.com/group/androgynes/surveys?id=868988

xxxMOTIVATION & EMOTION. Retrieved September 16, 2008. http://www.alleydog.com/101notes/mot-emot.html

Motivation and Emotion . Retrieved September 16, 2008. http://allpsych.com/psychology101/motivation.html

Wikipedia: Motivation. Retrieved September 16, 2008. http://en.wikipedia.org/wiki/Motivation

xxxiRetrieved from Susans.org on September 9, 2008 from topic poll http://www.susans.org/forums/index.php/topic,17184.0.html
Poll started by Nero. Includes suggestions from Tay, No_id, Pica Pica, Rebis, Laurry, and myself.

xxxiihttp://radicalbitch.wordpress.com/2009/01/09/magical-thinking-extreme-ego-defense-and-sociopathic-behaviour/

xxxiii The Importance of Given Names by Donna Przecha http://www.genealogy.com/35_donna.html

xxxivGender-Free Pronouns http://www.bbc.co.uk/dna/h2g2/A770960

xxxv androgyne. (n.d.). *Dictionary.com Unabridged (v 1.1)*. Retrieved September 05, 2008, from Dictionary.com website: http://dictionary.reference.com/browse/androgyne

xxxvi andro-. (n.d.). *Dictionary.com Unabridged (v 1.1)*. Retrieved September 05, 2008, from Dictionary.com website: http://dictionary.reference.com/browse/andro-

xxxvii gyneco-. (n.d.). *Dictionary.com Unabridged (v 1.1)*. Retrieved September 05, 2008, from Dictionary.com website: http://dictionary.reference.com/browse/gyneco-

xxxviii androgyne. (n.d.). *Dictionary.com Unabridged (v 1.1)*. Retrieved September 05, 2008, from Dictionary.com website: http://dictionary.reference.com/browse/androgyne

xxxixSee discussion in the post concerning uses of Androgyne in the "Possible Preface to an androgyne book" post at Whatisgender.net.
http://www.whatisgender.net/phpBB3/viewtopic.php?f=147&t=1373

xl From Abstract at CAT.INIST.FR Mutations of the androgyne: Its functions in early modern French literature = Les mutations de l'androgyne : Ses fonctions dans la littérature de la Renaissance website
http://cat.inist.fr/?aModele=afficheN&cpsidt=15102560

xli How do you feel about your gender? [Poll]. Retrieved September 13, 2008 from Androgynes Yahoo Group
http://groups.yahoo.com/group/androgynes/surveys?id=492177

xlii Questions about sex, androgyny and religion. [Poll]. Retrieved September13, 2008 from Androgynes Yahoo Group http://groups.yahoo.com/group/androgynes/surveys?id=650524

xliiiHow are you feel you are usually preceived in your daily life interacting with society in general? [Poll]. Retrieved September 13, 2008 from Androgynes Yahoo Group
http://groups.yahoo.com/group/androgynes/surveys?id=915034

xlivBased on recent discussions I was wondering as androgynes if our heights were skewed from the traditional shorter females & taller males such as more shorter birth males & taller birth females? Please pick birth sex & closest height combination! [Poll]. Retrieved September 13, 2008 from Androgynes Yahoo Group
http://groups.yahoo.com/group/androgynes/surveys?id=1171351

xlv Do you believe in a binary gender system. Retrieved September 30, 2008 from IFGE.org
http://ifge.org/Poll-3results.phtml
xlviUK Population Estimate. https://www.cia.gov/library/publications/the-world-factbook/print/uk.html

xlviiCanada Population Clock. http://www.statcan.ca/english/edu/clock/population.htm

xlviiiAustralia Population Clock. http://www.abs.gov.au/ausstats/abs
%40.nsf/94713ad445ff1425ca25682000192af2/1647509ef7e25faaca2568a900154b63?
OpenDocument

xlix laura's playground, taken 5/12/11 from http://www.lauras-playground.com/forums/
index.php?showtopic=8267

xlx poll retrieved May 13, 2011 from http://www.susans.org/forums/index.php
/topic,96905.0/viewresults.html

Sociology

social psychology- conformity, discrimination, cognitive dissonance

discrimination

marginalizing, pushed aside – 14

society & culture looks down on gender exploration – 19

"this-is-not-that" leads to discrimination - 22

speaking up

non-binary voice-issues, presence, understanding, respect, equality, awareness-5

remaining silent instead of going against society – 8

knowledge of = first step to discussion, issues, research - 17

being different

diversity (named & unnamed) – 7

awareness of being different than others (not fitting in) - 7

suppression, try to fit in (try to hide, forget, change, or replace) – 7

troubles socially, fake fitting in, awkwardness, inhibitions, overacting – 8

social agents- parents, teachers, religious figures, relatives, neighbors, and peers

enforce gender behavior , direct or indirect, force inhibitions, ought & should-19

feel ought to be certain gender way, social agent pressures & expectations - 20

ideal, ought selves

social agents enforce gender behavior, also create "should s" - 19

social rewards: praise, recognition, social status – 19

avoid social punishments of ridicule, violence, feelings of being low status, picked on, or feeling of being wrong – 19

feel ought to be certain gender way, social agent pressures & expectations - 20

rare and uncommon

rare and uncommon, feeling lost, can't talk to other gender persons – 7

relationships- love, attraction, desire, orientations

Self-concept and Personal Growth
self-concept or self-schema
> collection of the aspects of the self-identity - 19

self-esteem- self worth
> high fake self, low true self - 8

false and true selves- deceit
> everything you have learned your whole life from others, about you and the world, seems wrong - 9
>
> living a lie, less satisfaction, more pain & discomfort, low esteem – 20
>
> untangle web; deceit, suppression,dissonance, and discrepancies= true self - 20

self-discrepancies- current/actual, ideal [hopes, dreams, wishes] (motivates individuals to change, improve and achieve), ought selves [obligations, duties, responsibilities]
> self into current, ideal, and ought selves – 19
>
> self vs ideal self image, one can experience great sadness, depression, dissatisfaction, and disappointment – 19
>
> self vs ought self one can experience anxiety, fear, pain, and discomfort – 19
>
> division selves common, non-binary first realizes gender discomfort – 20
>
> discrepancies in presentation - 41

cognitive dissonance- justifying, blaming, and denying of conflicting cognitive beliefs, attitudes, behaviors; a defense mechanisms

www.ingramcontent.com/pod-product-compliance
Lightning Source LLC
Chambersburg PA
CBHW070143290526
45789CB00002B/612